Glad to see you again
In this coloring book
there are no rules!
So let yourself enjoy
and color in any way
you wish to ^_^

Any questions? Email me
PawPrintTC@gmail.com

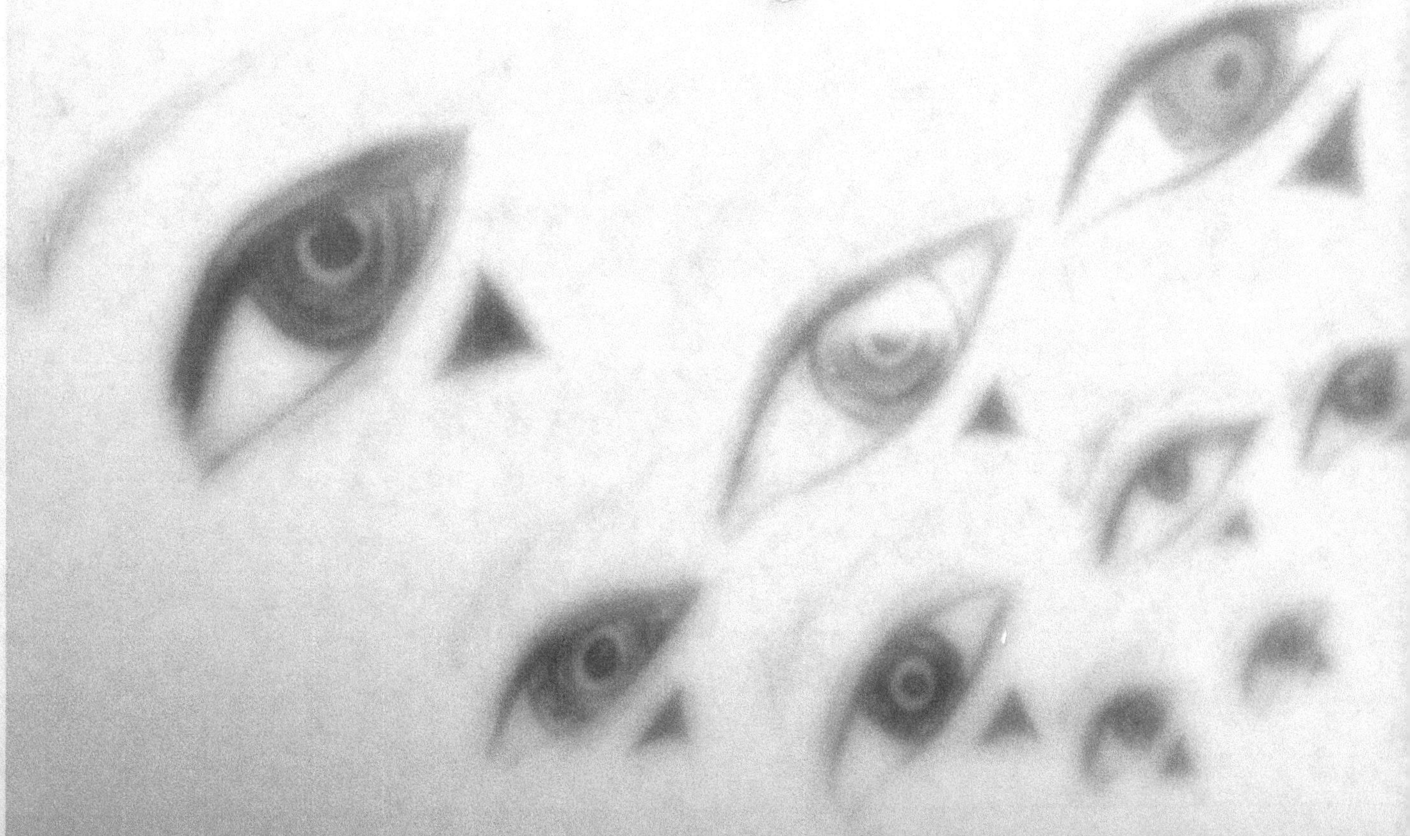

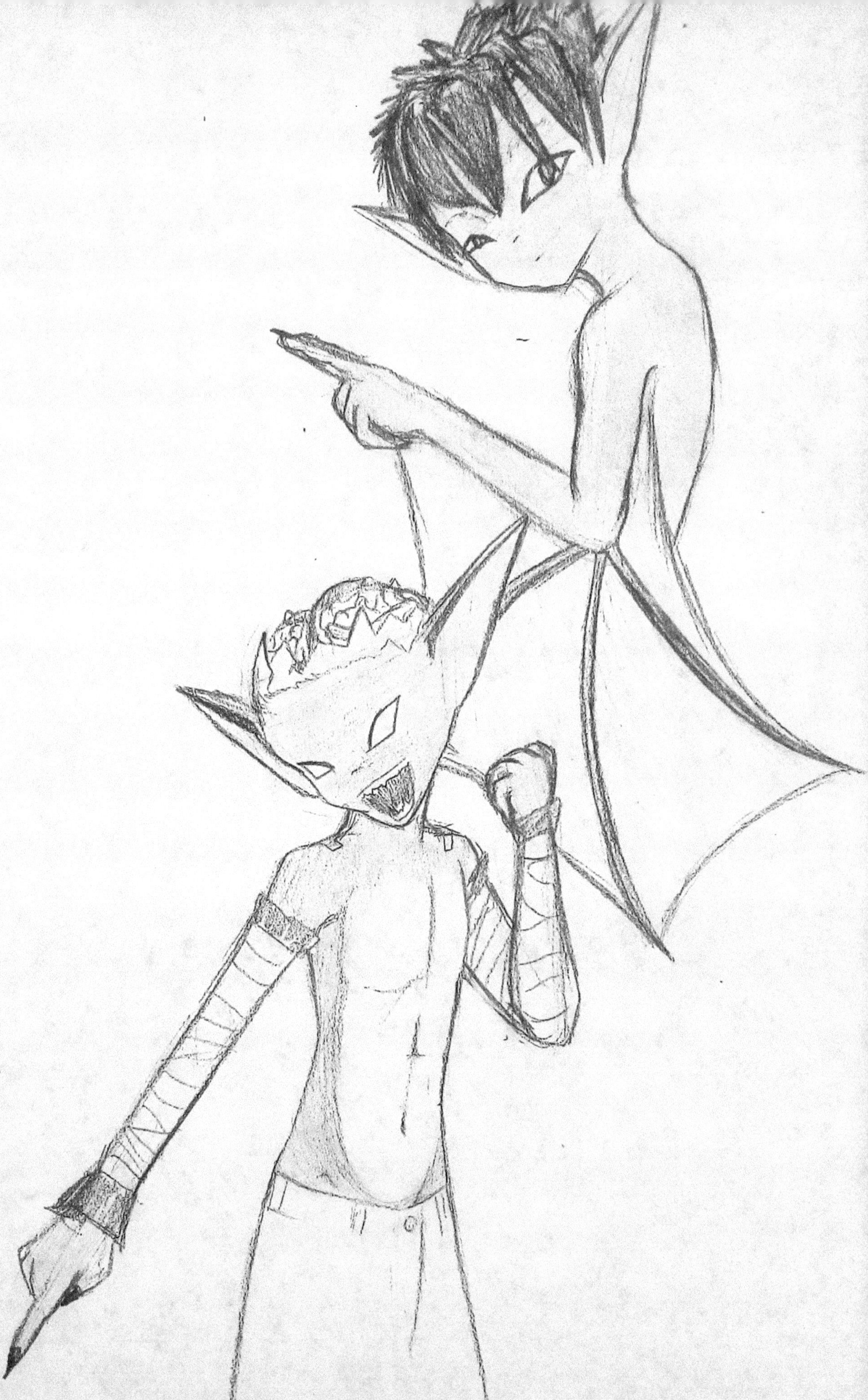

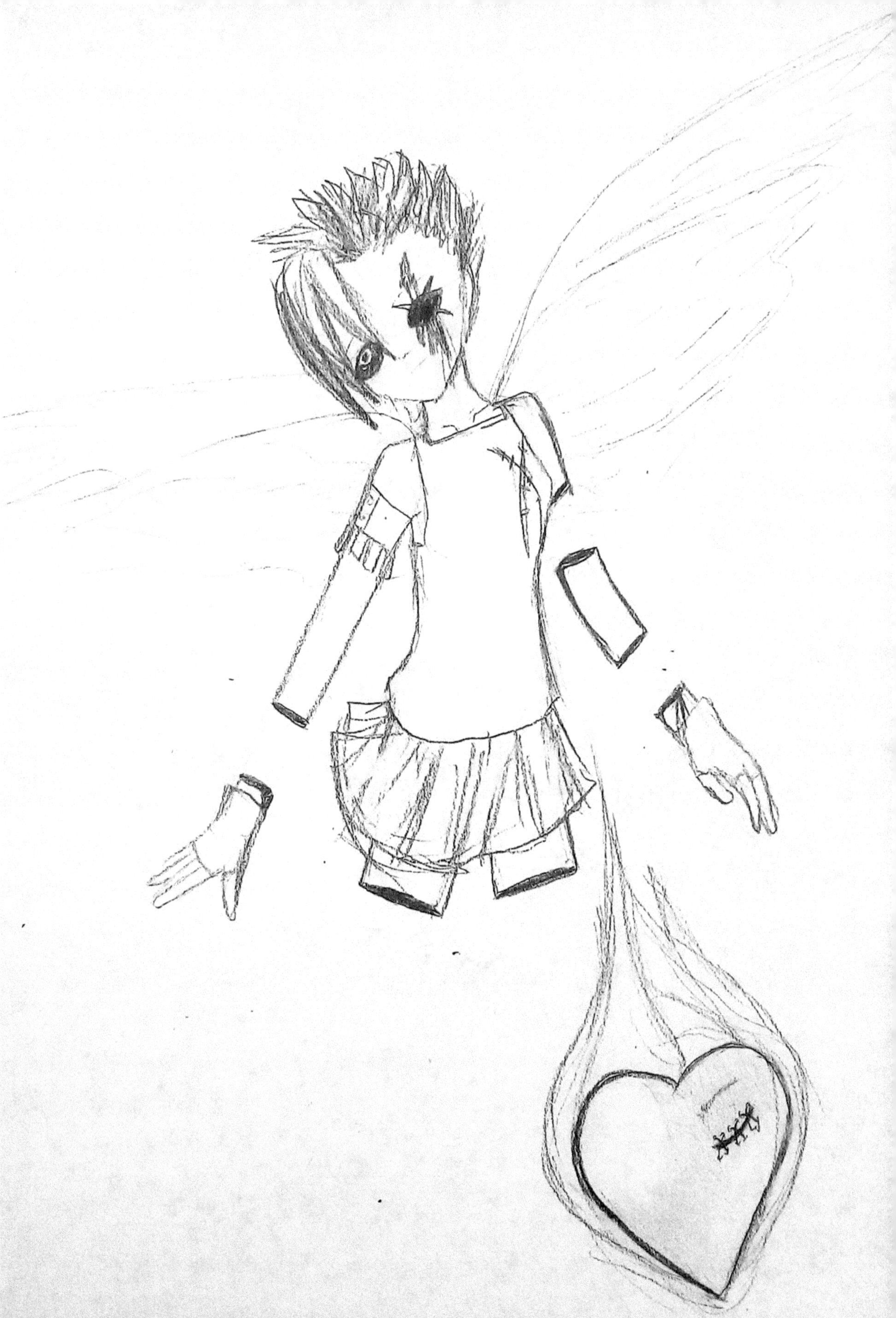

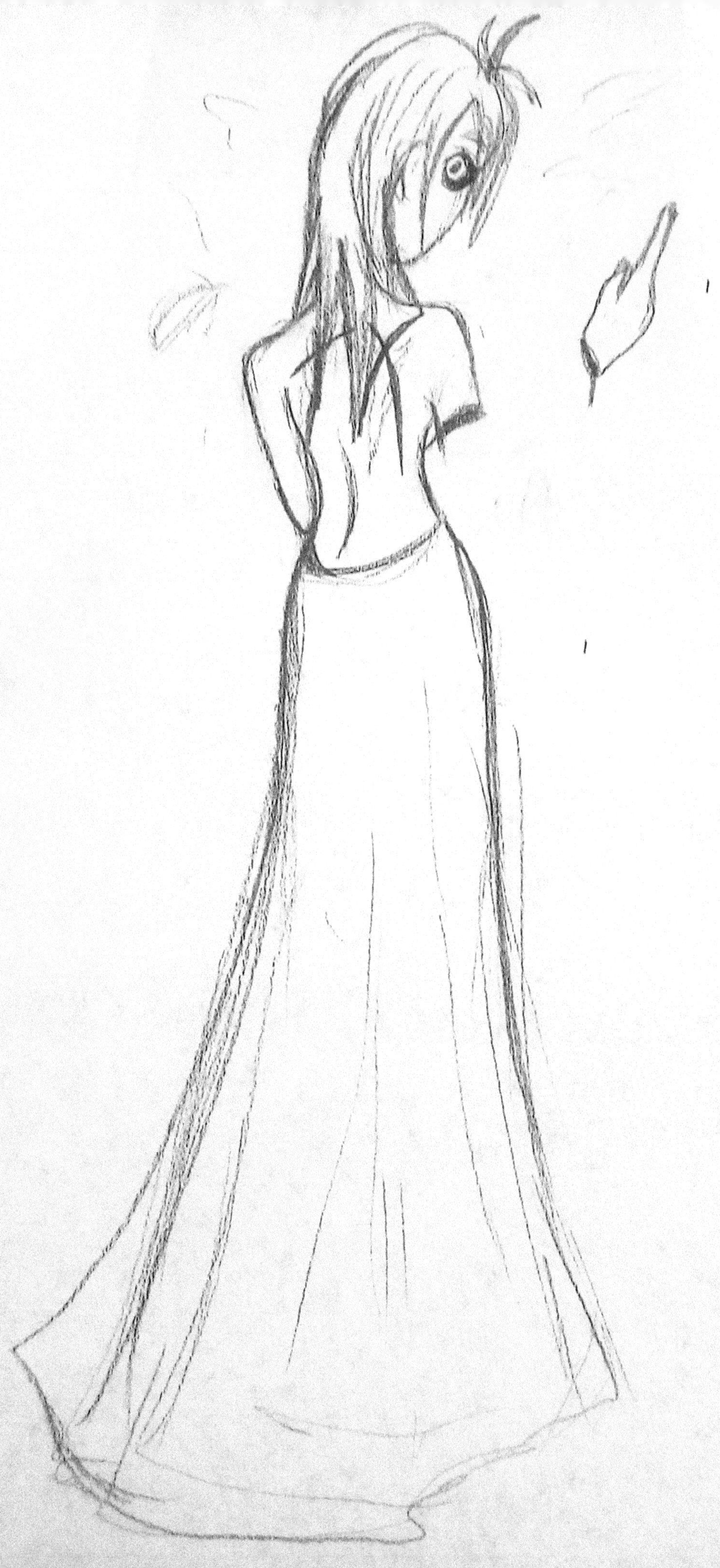

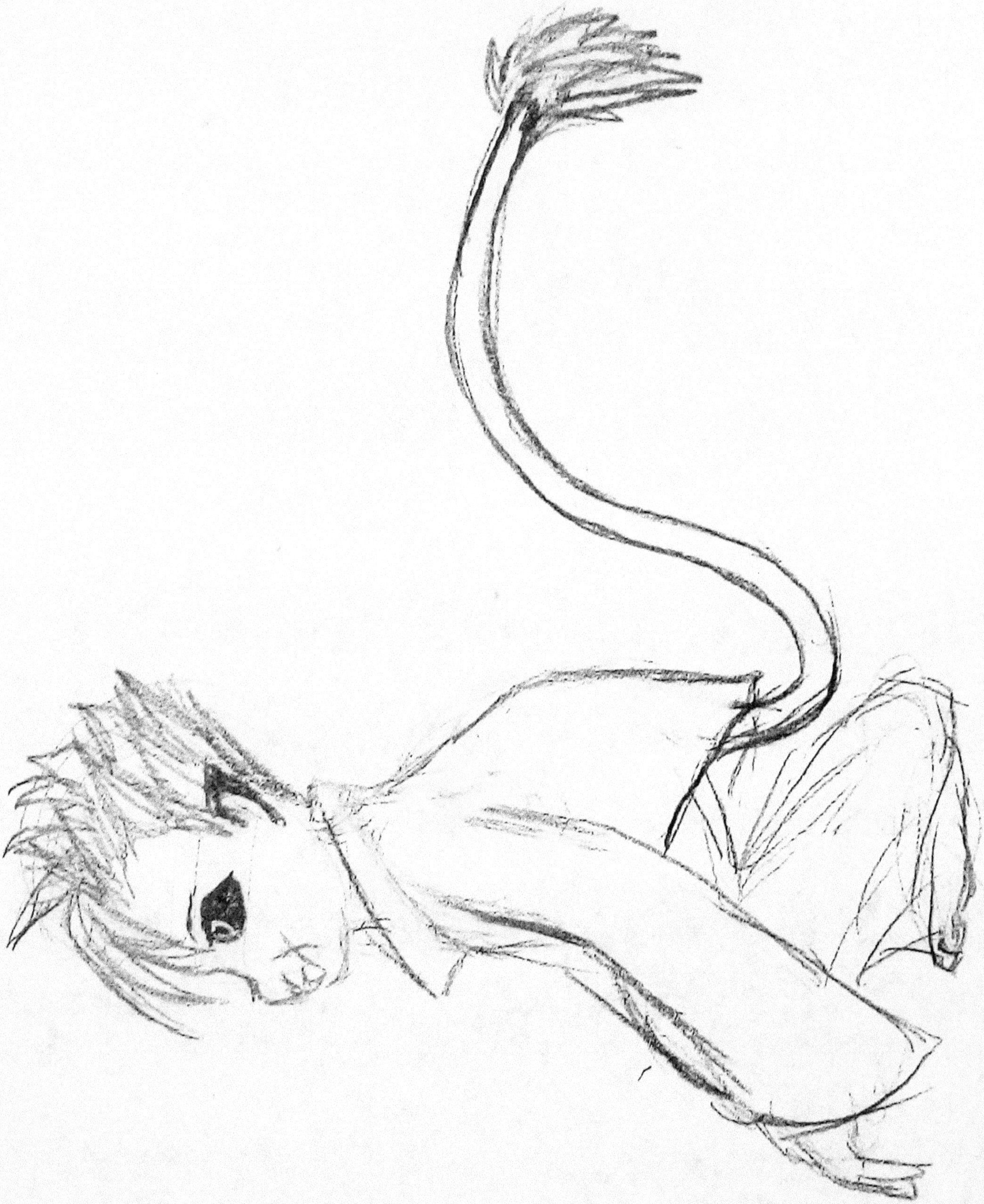

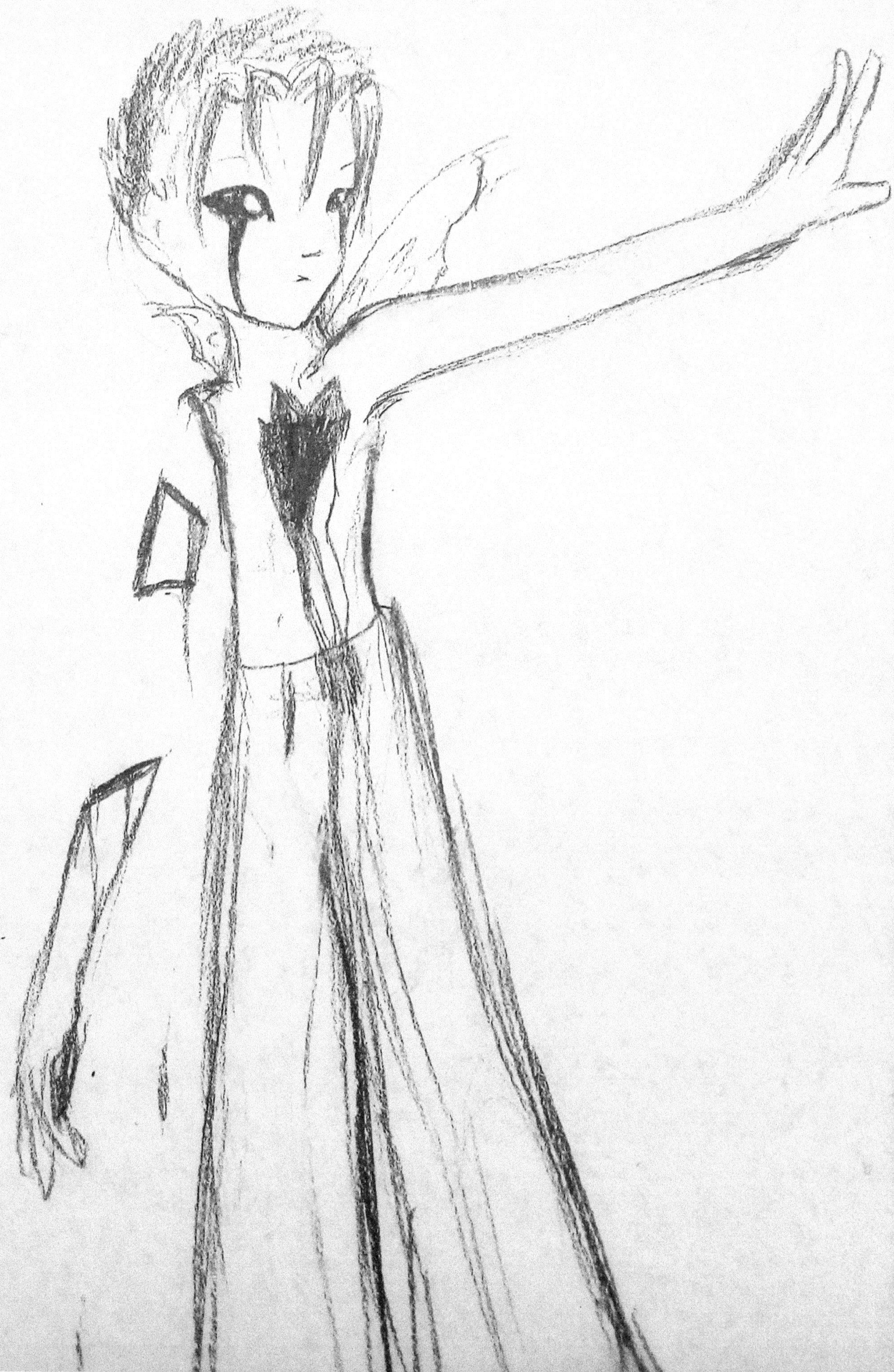

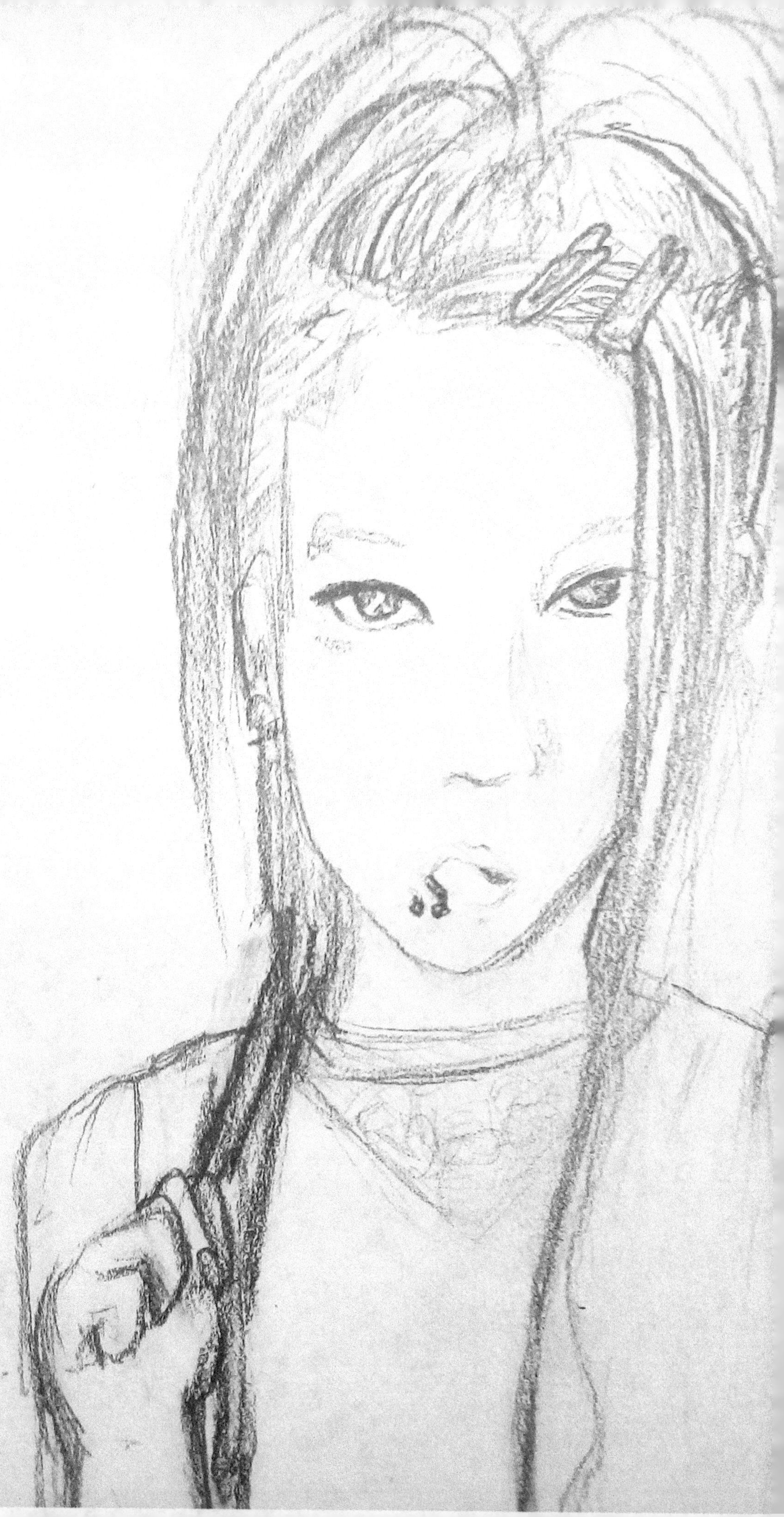

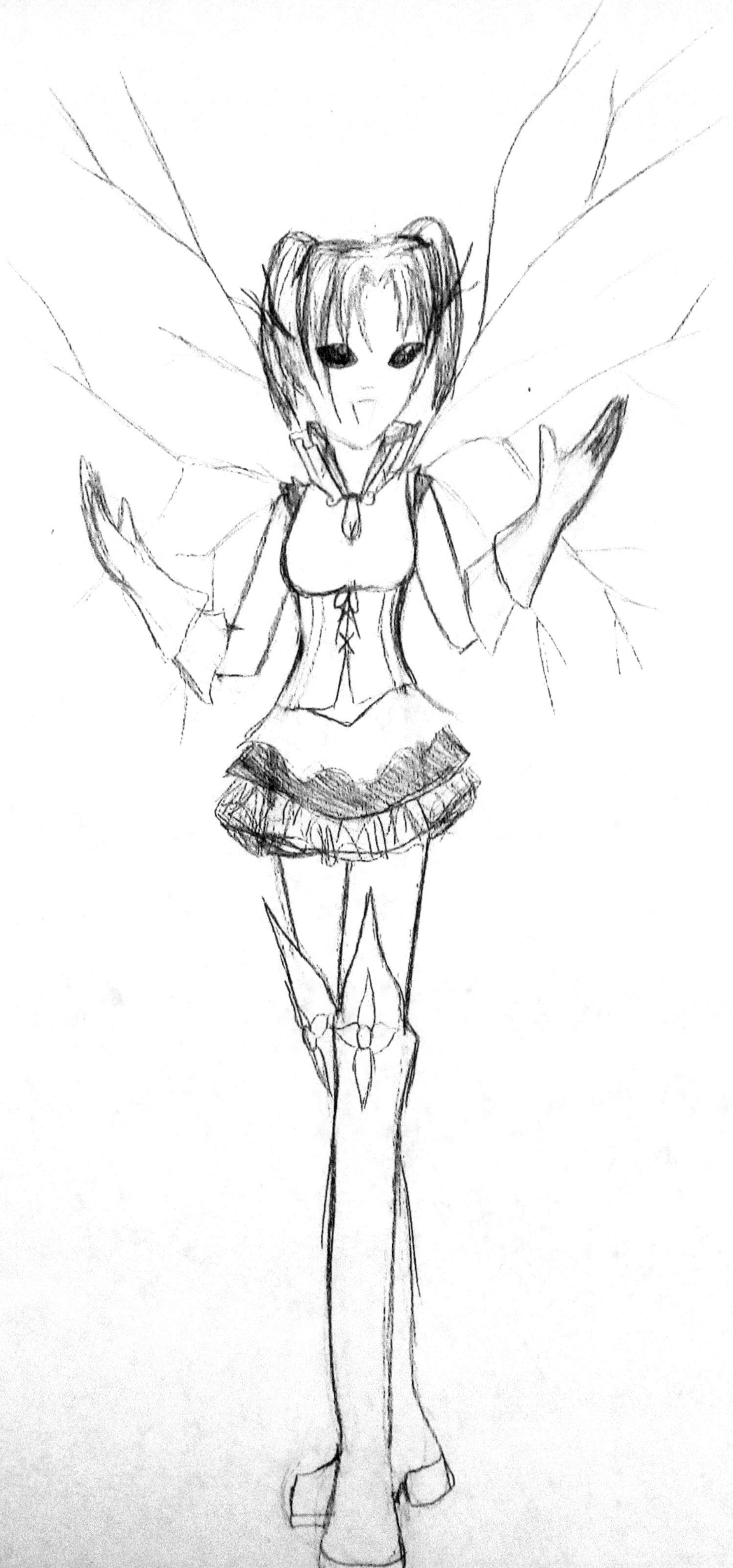

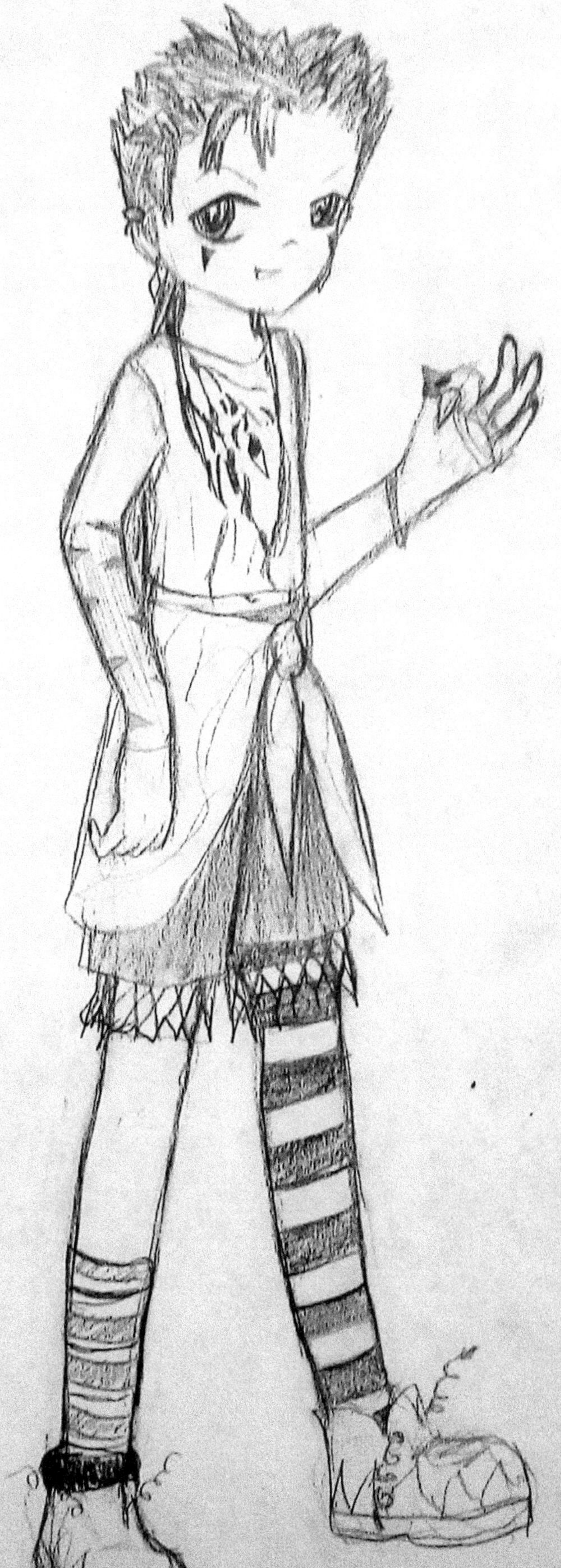

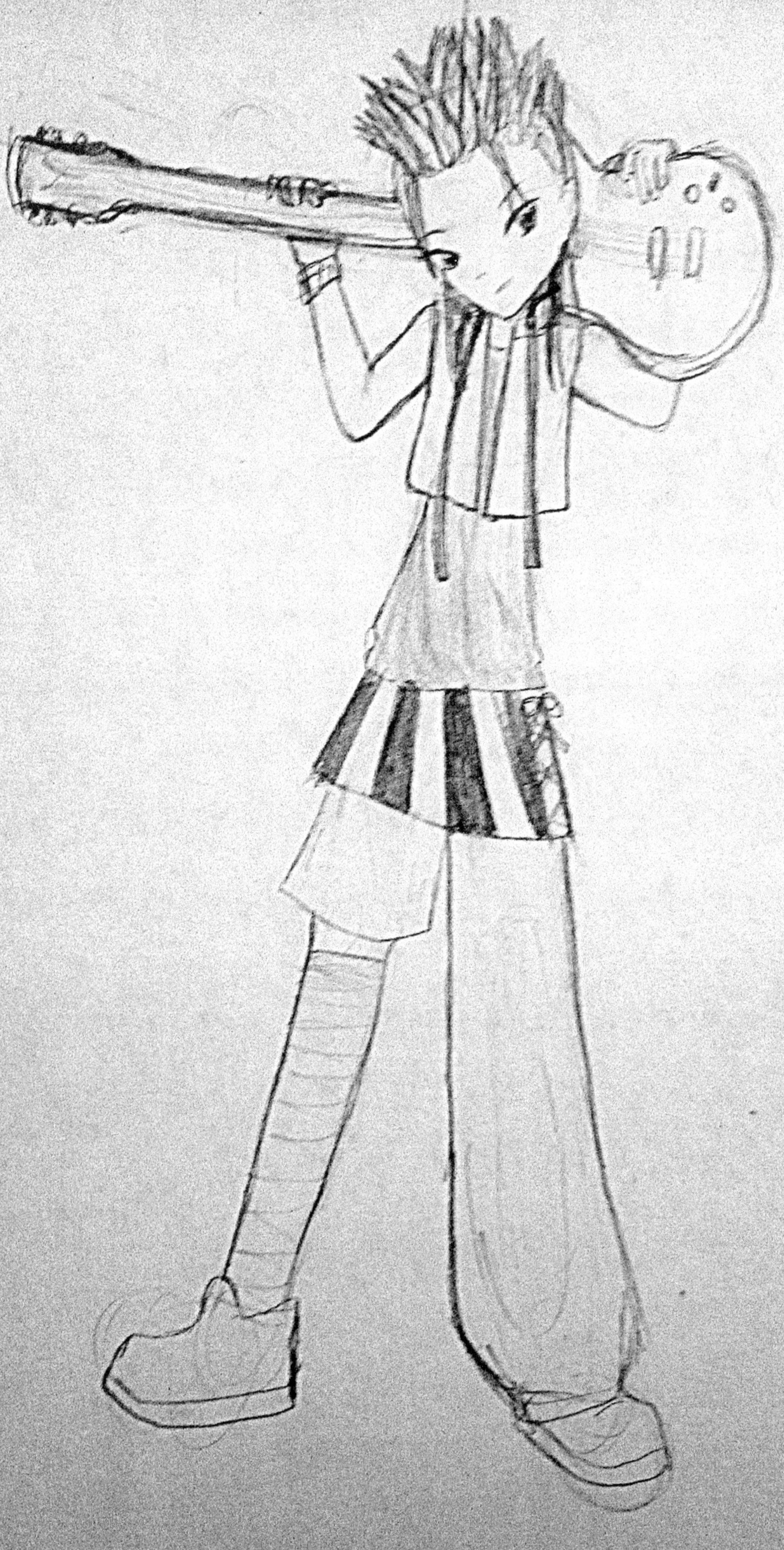

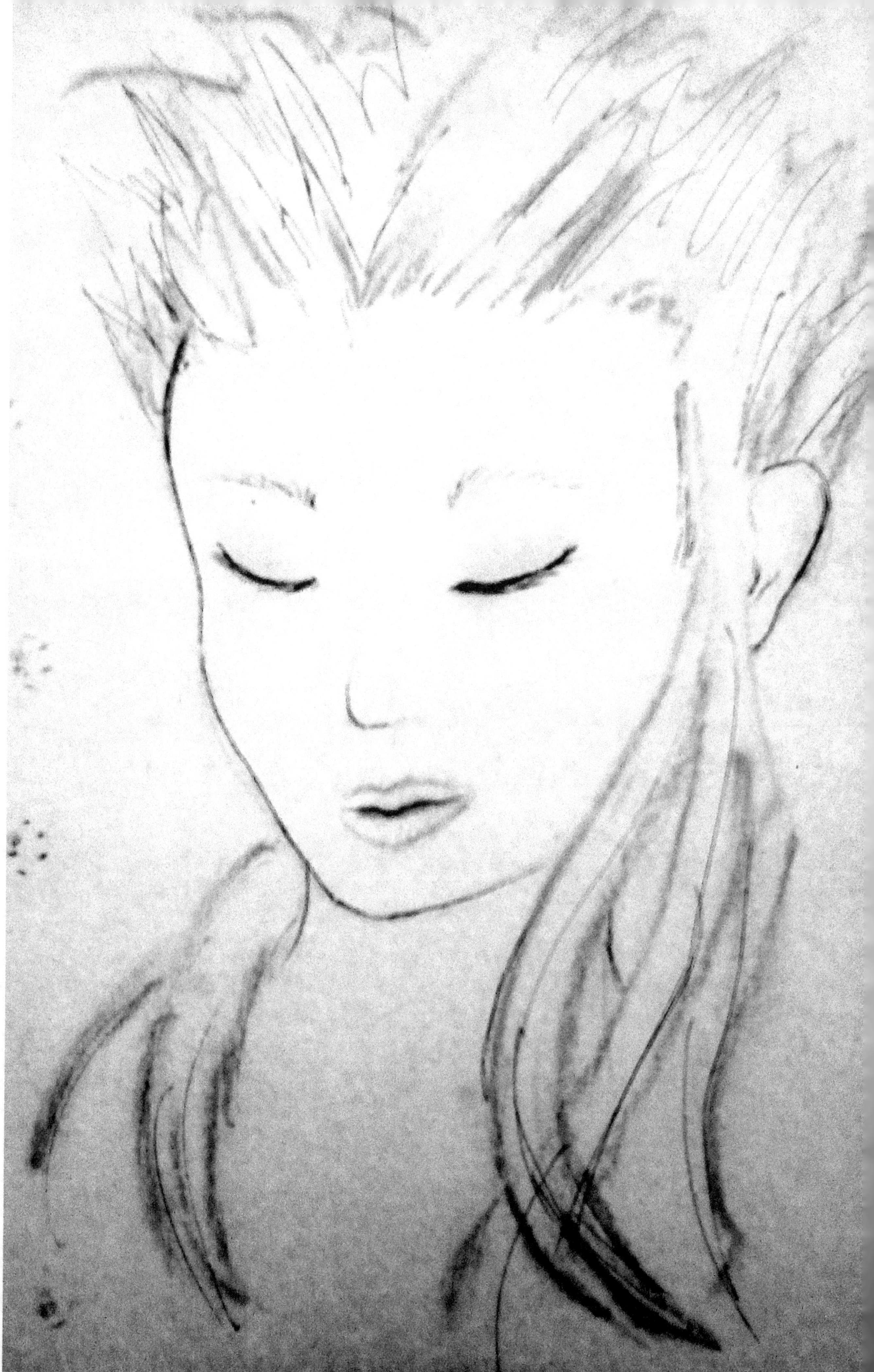

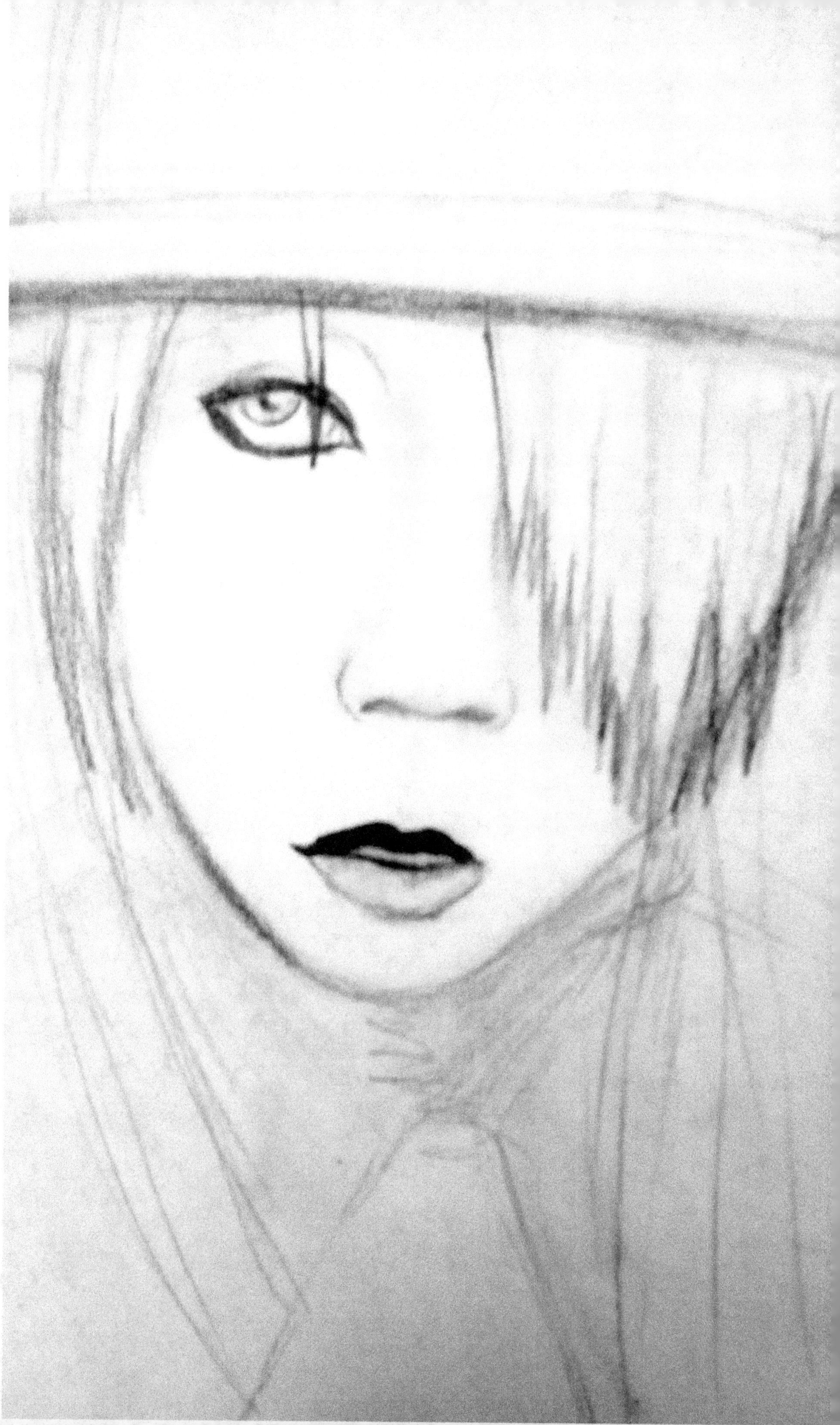

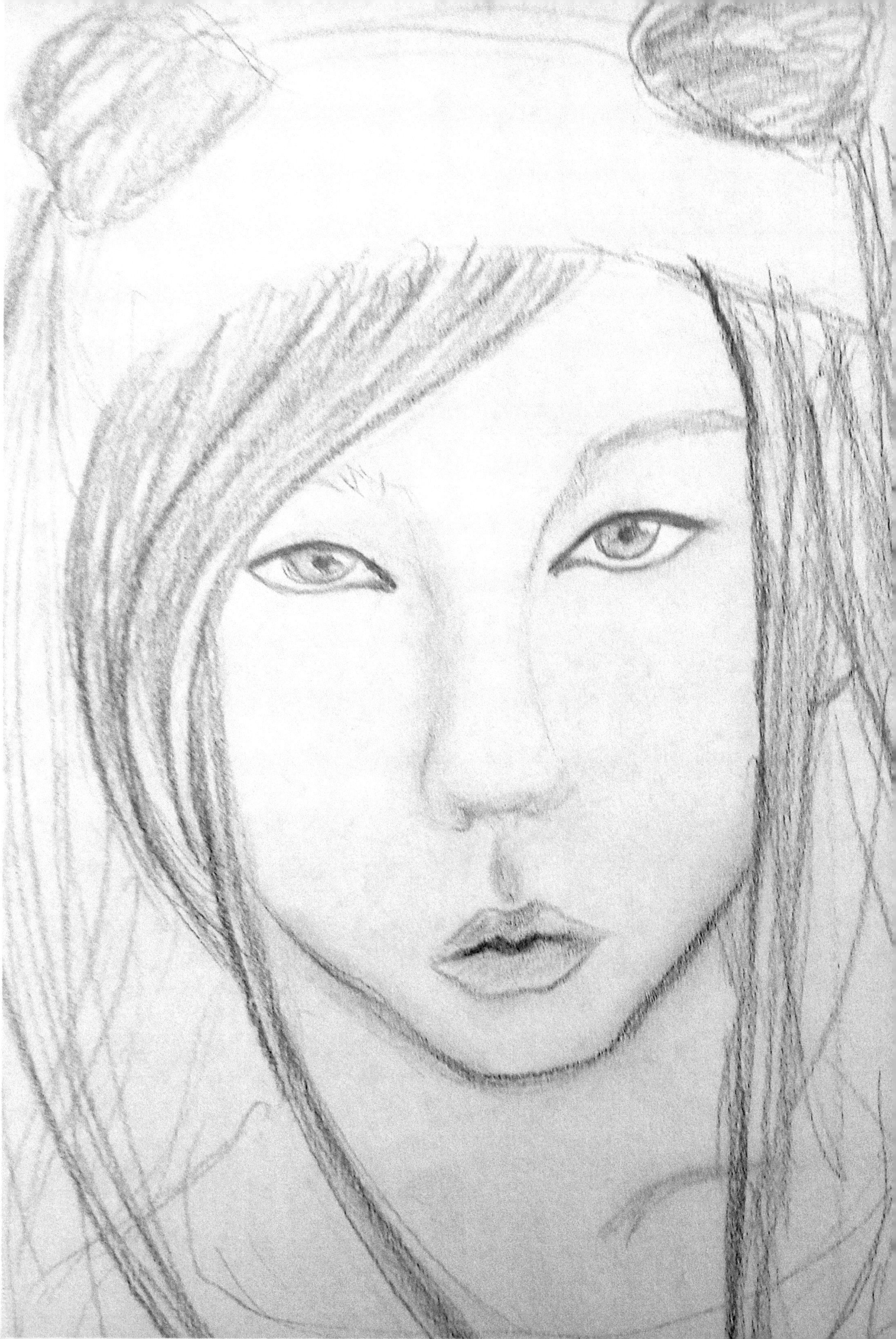

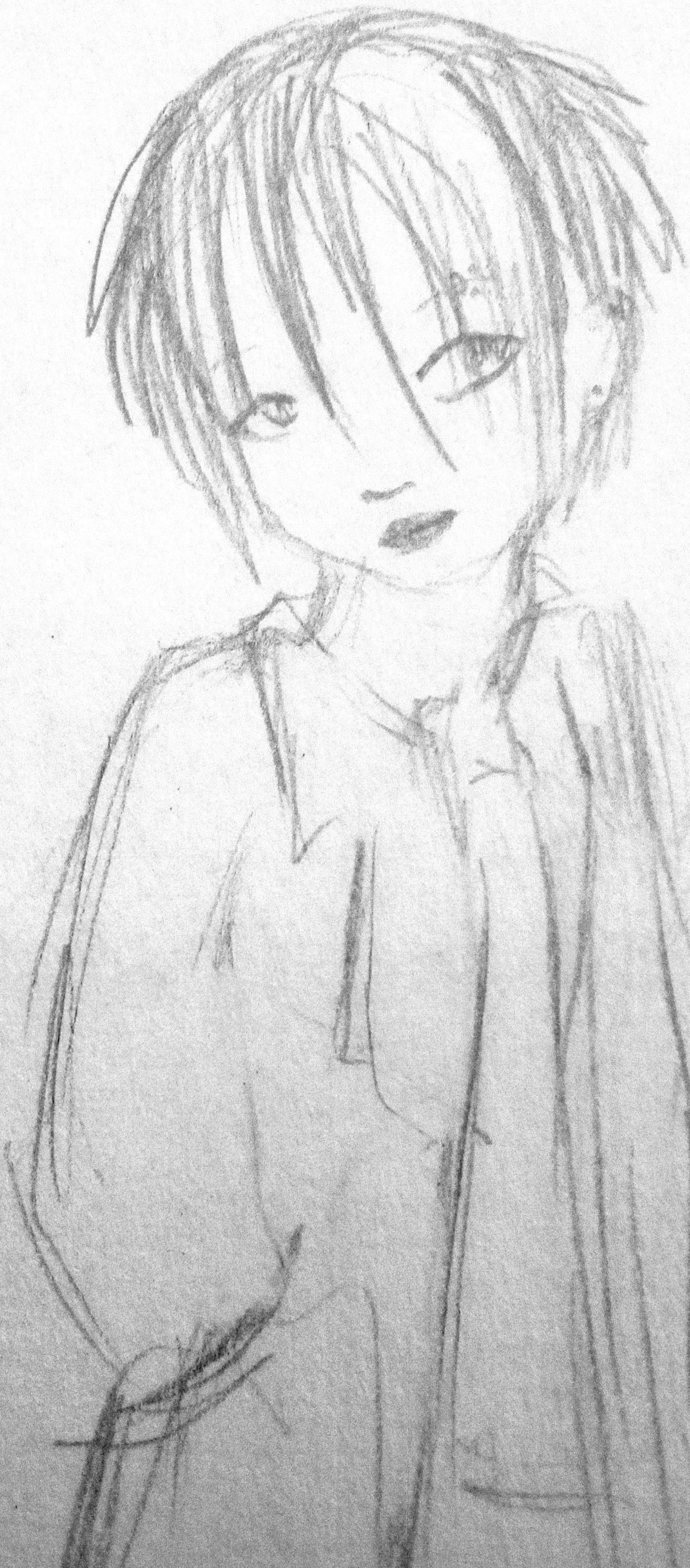

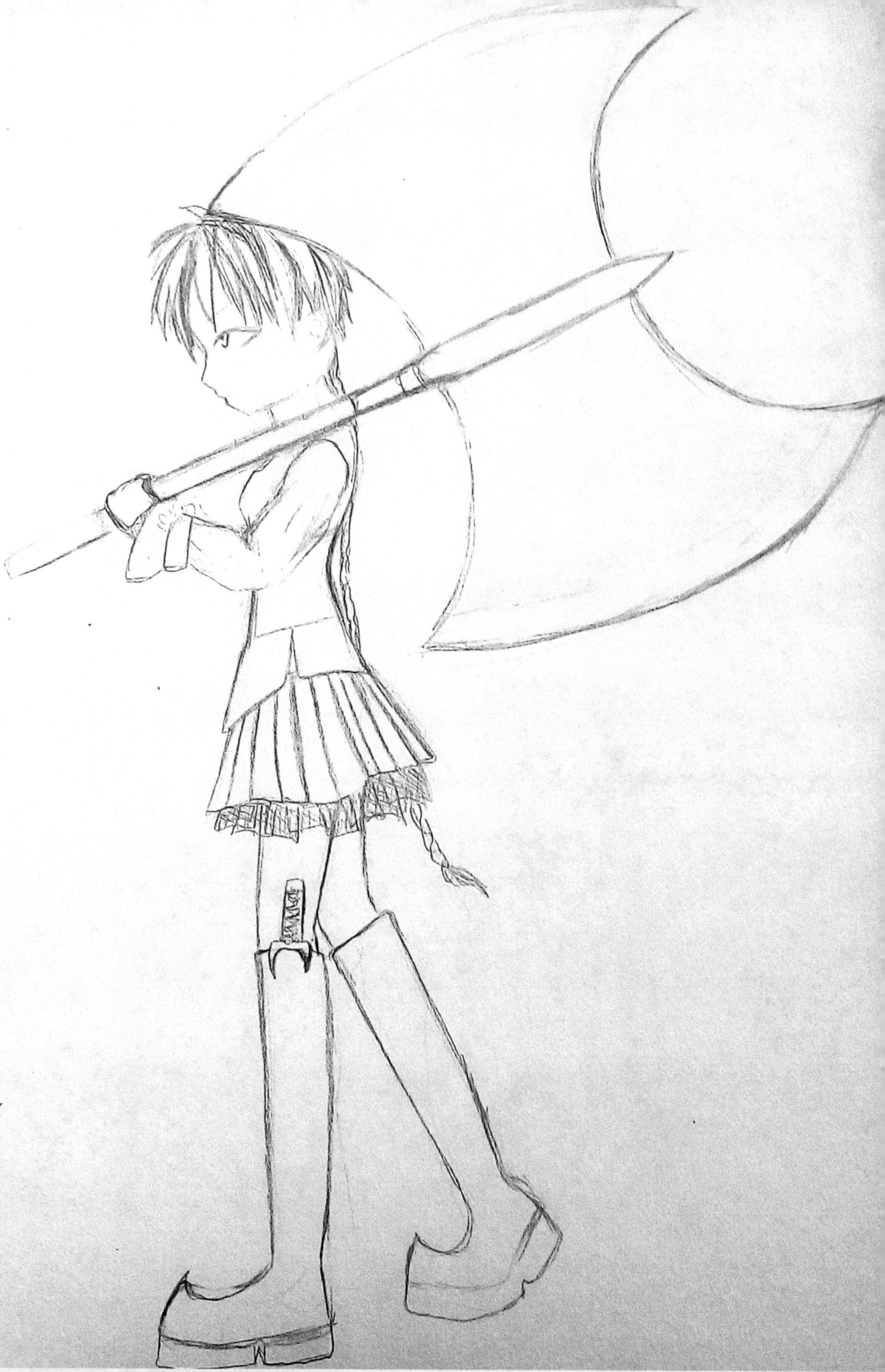

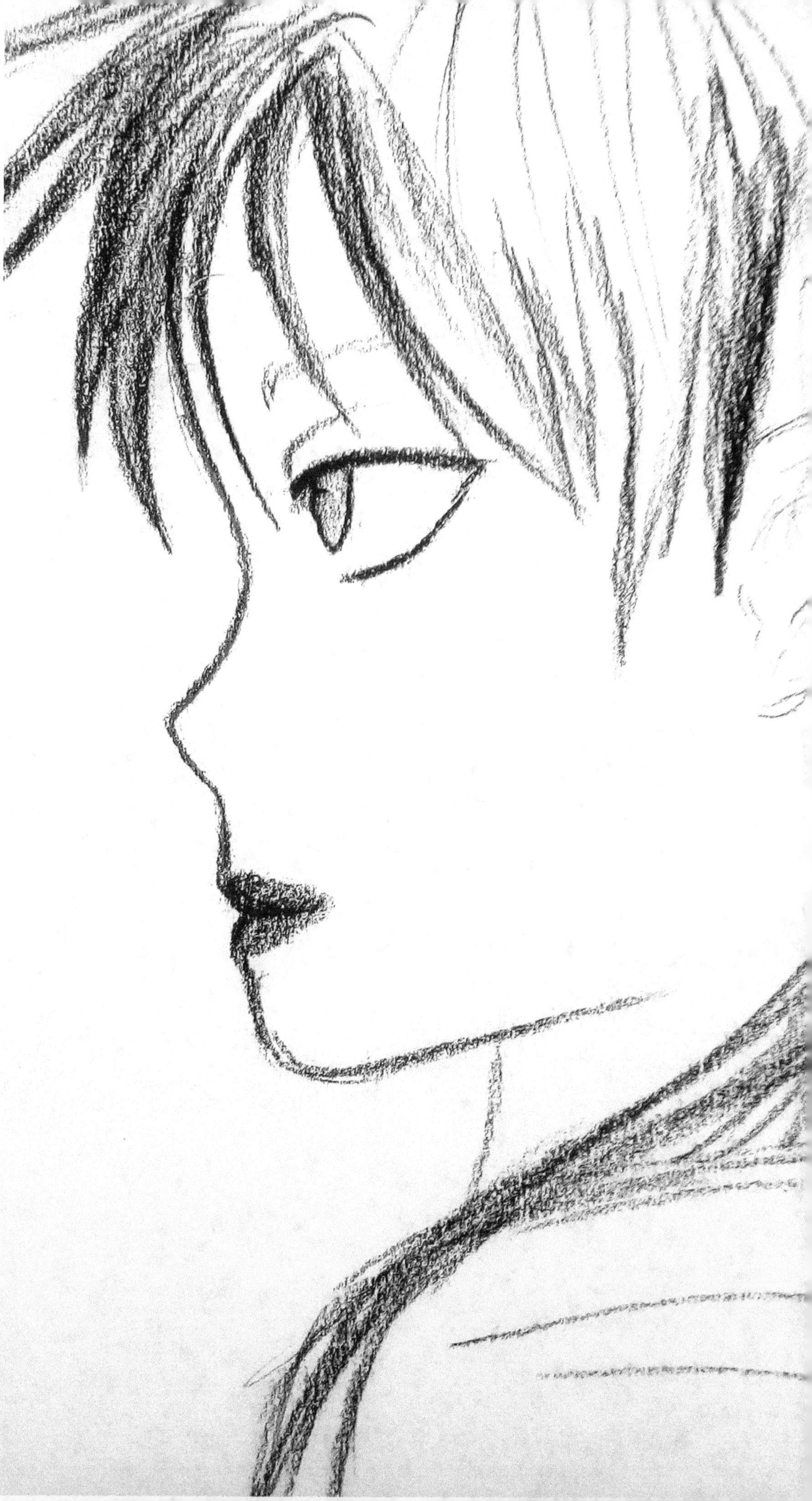

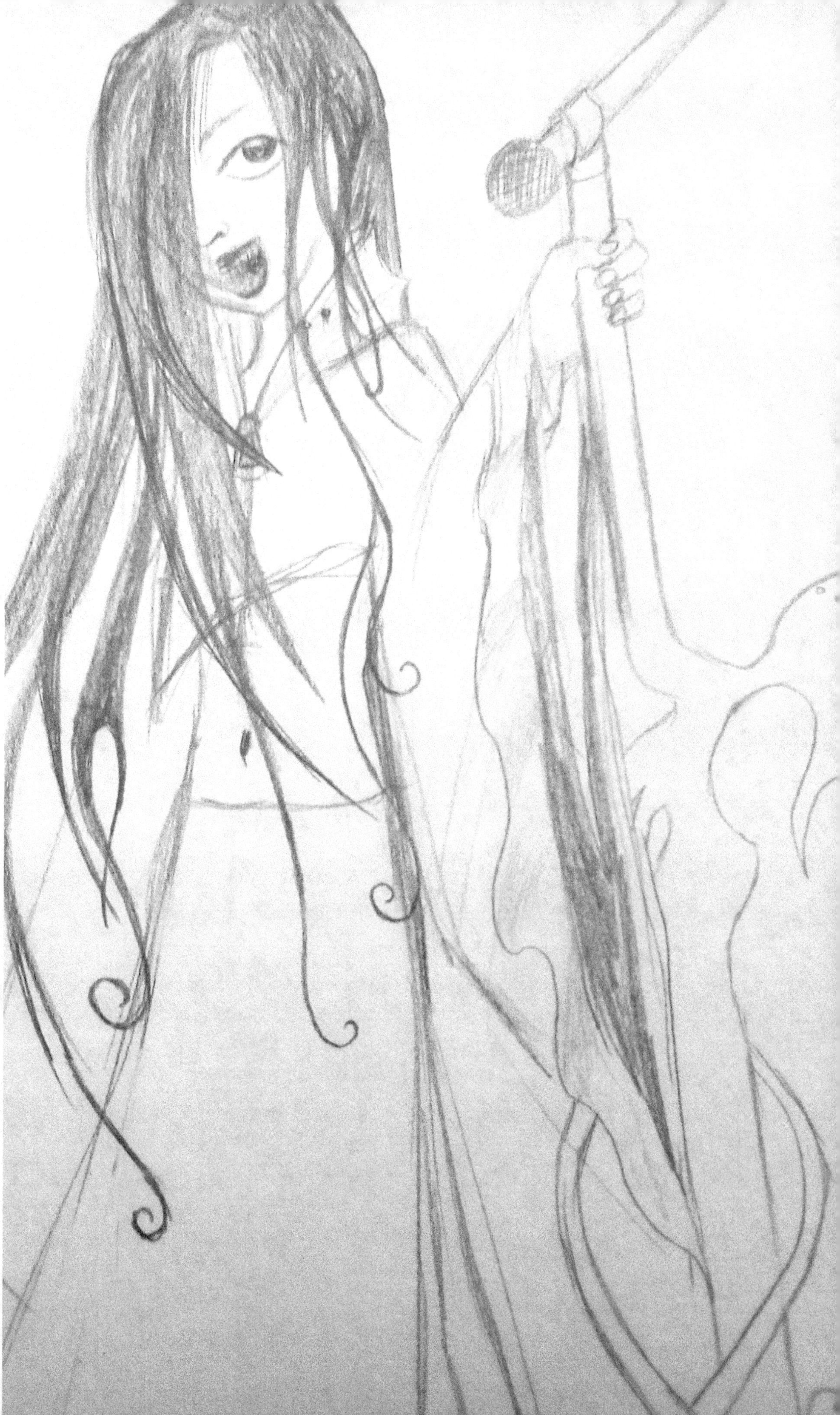

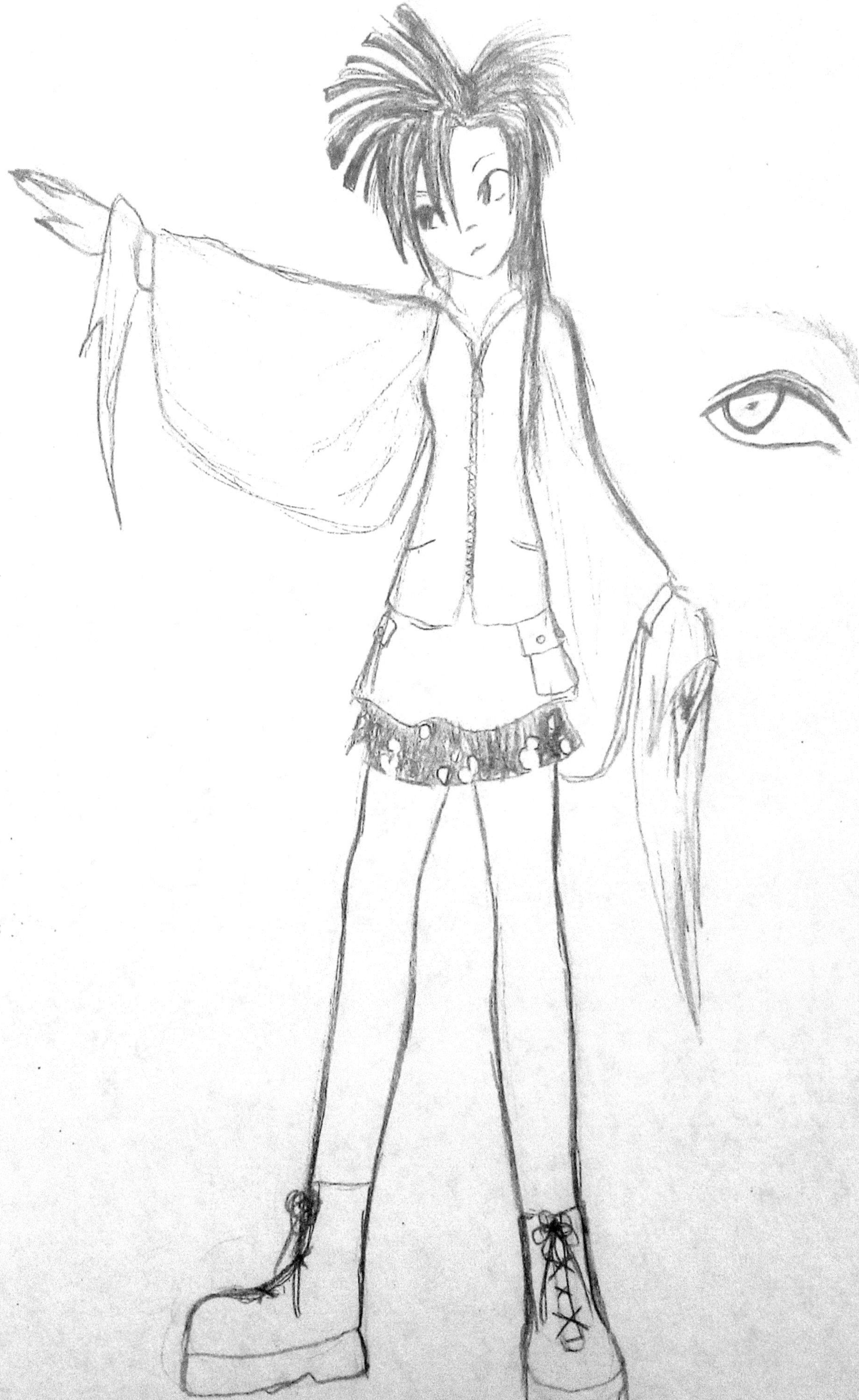

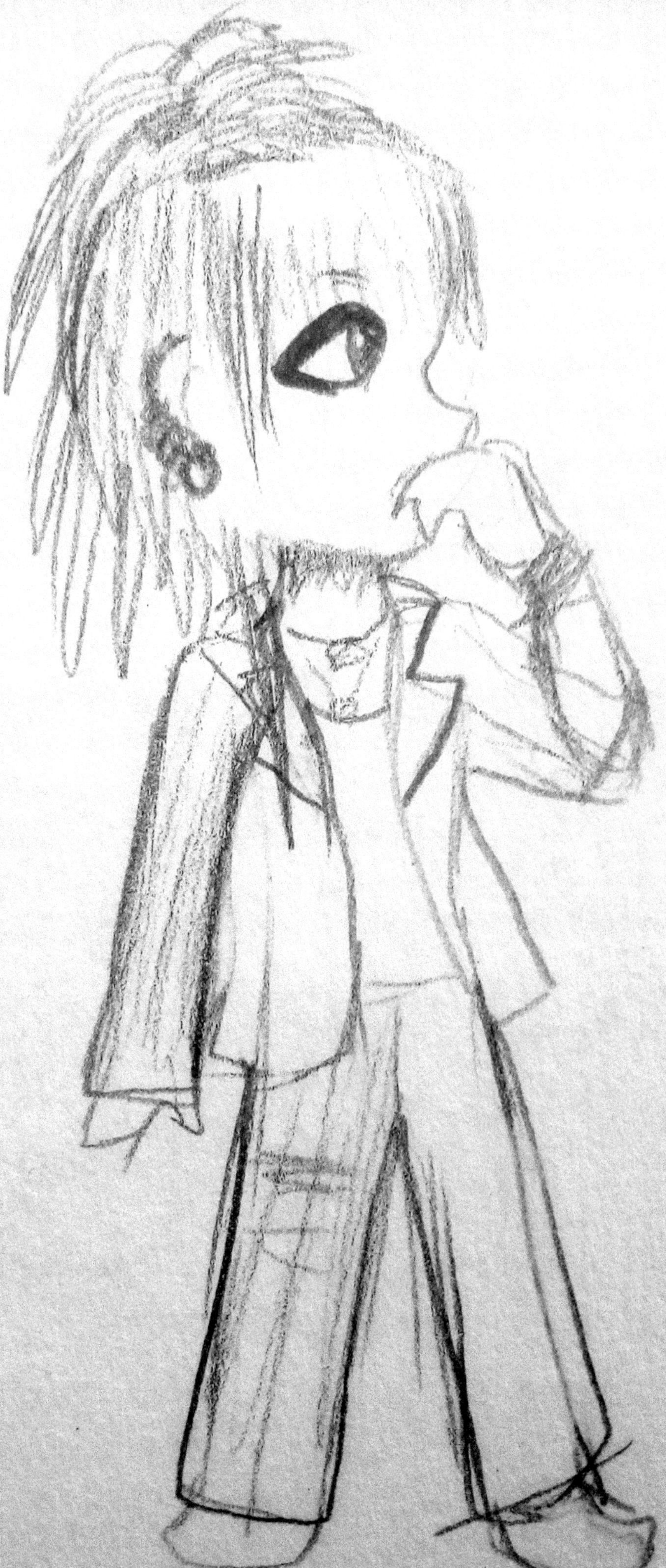

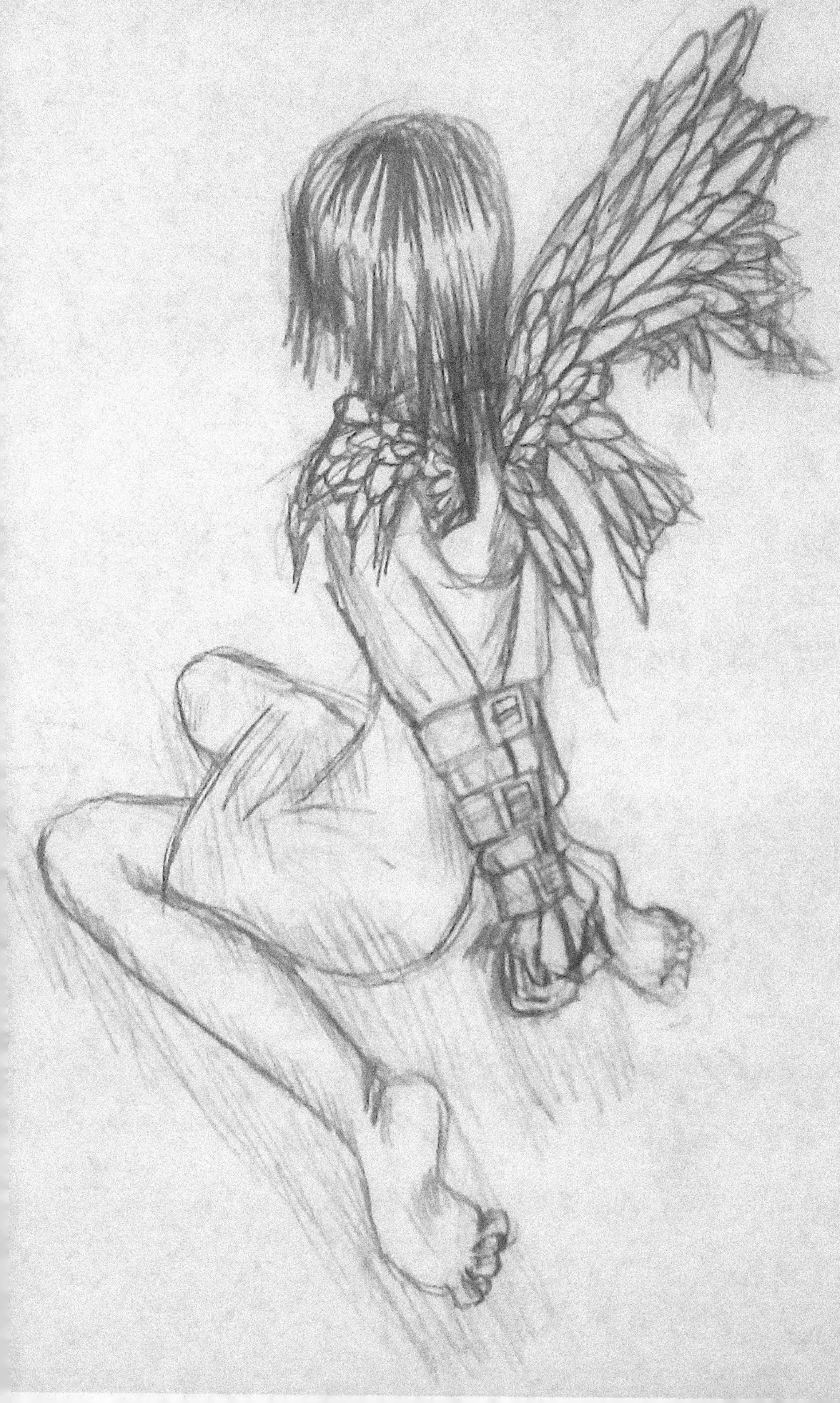

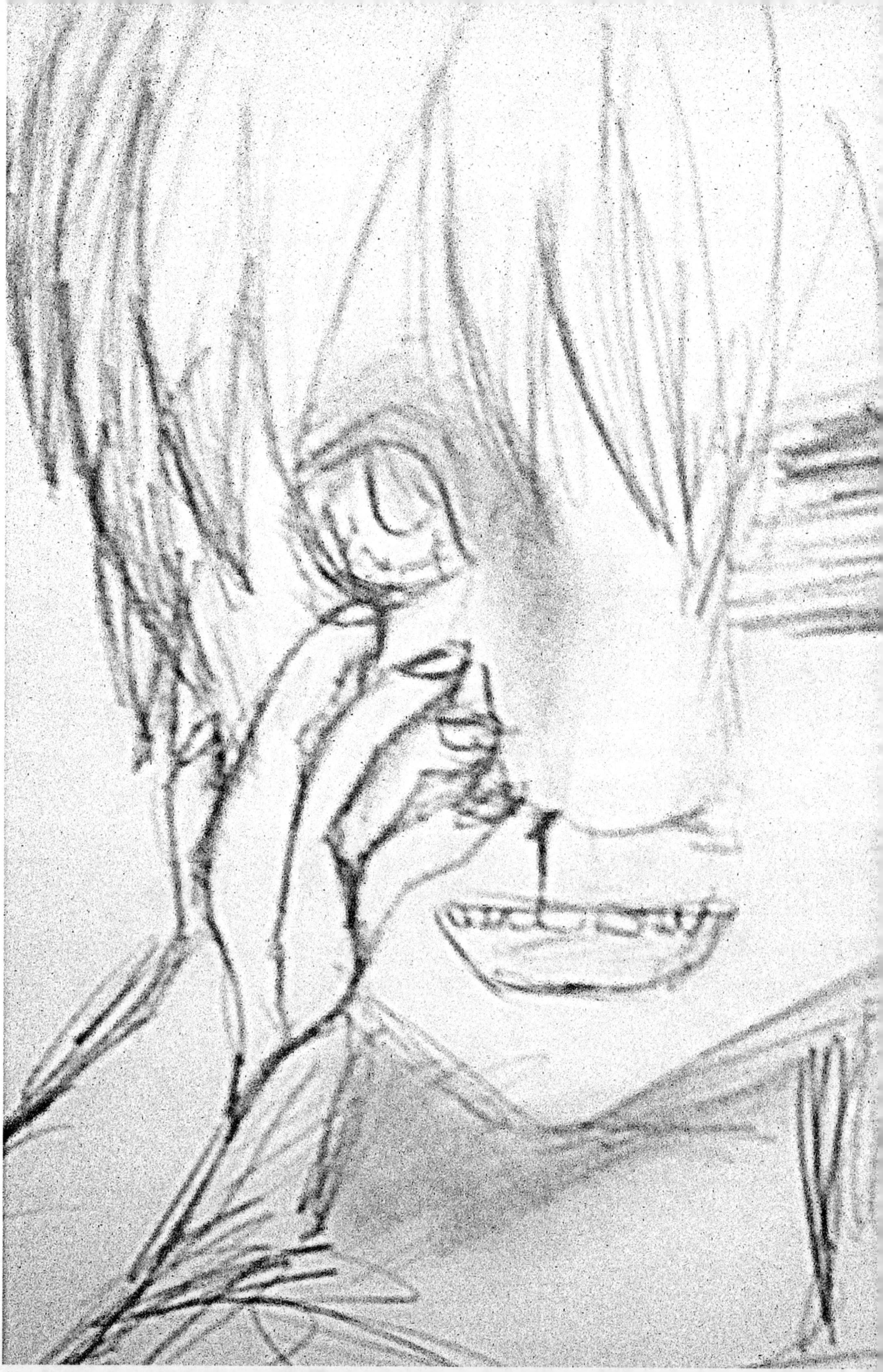

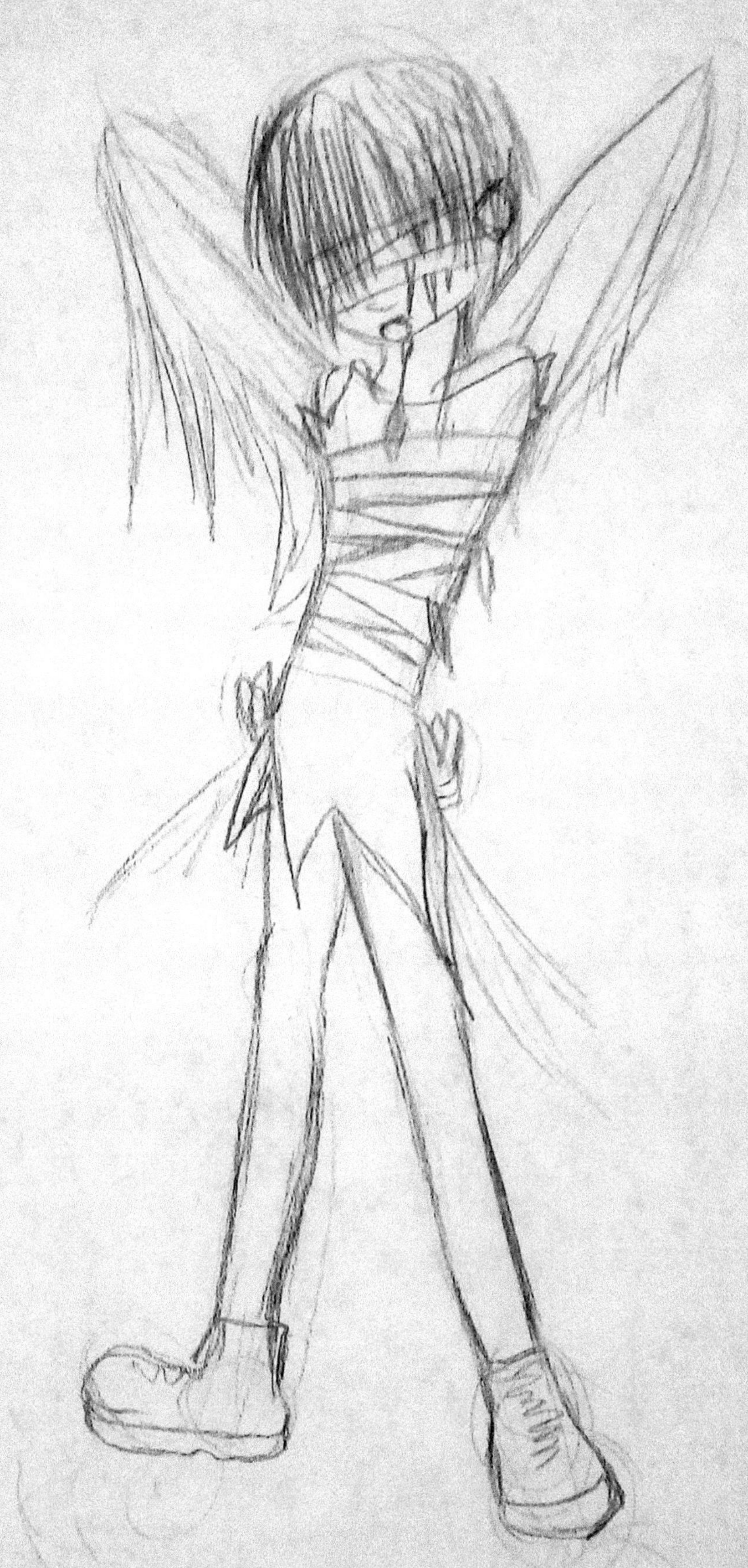

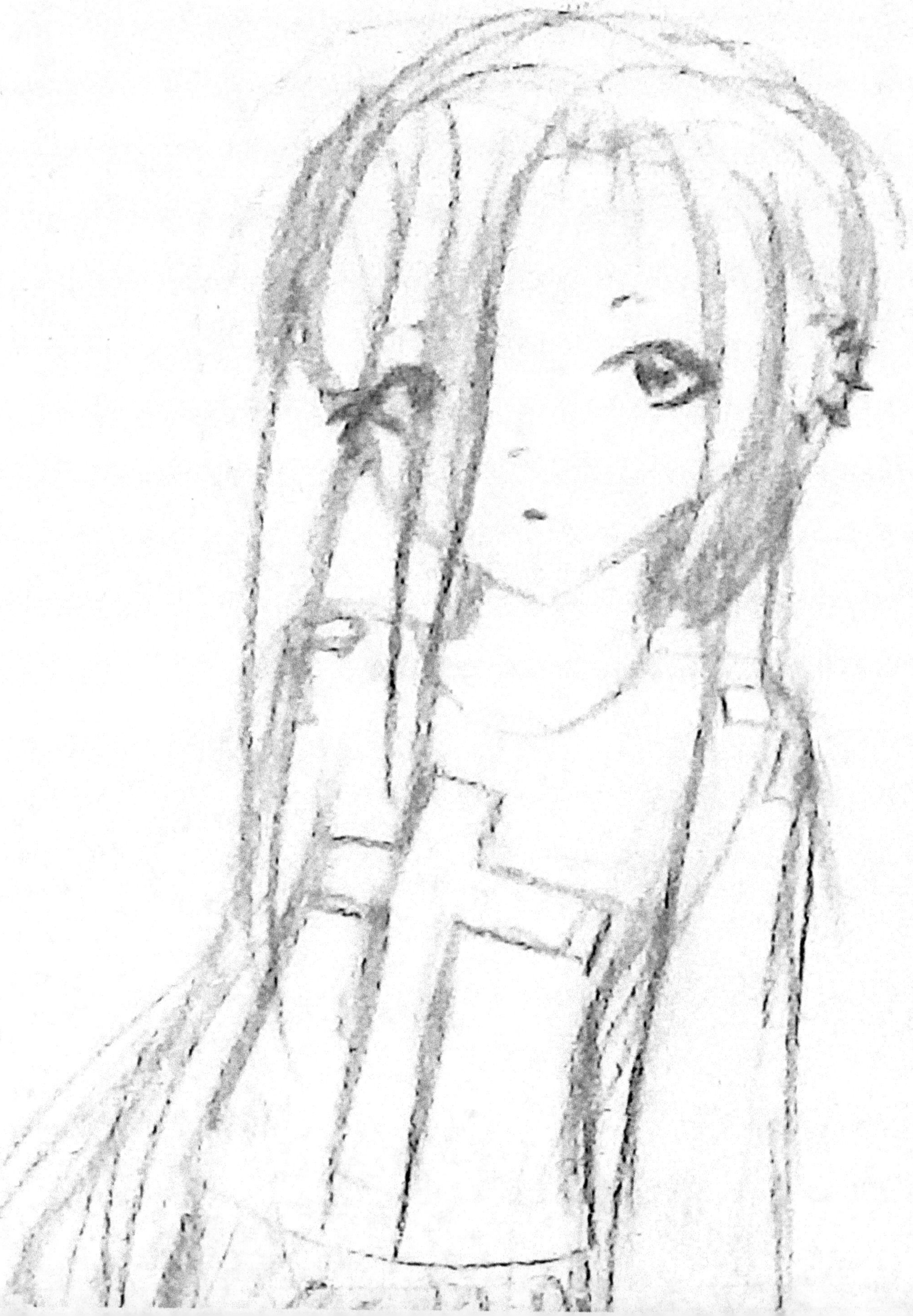

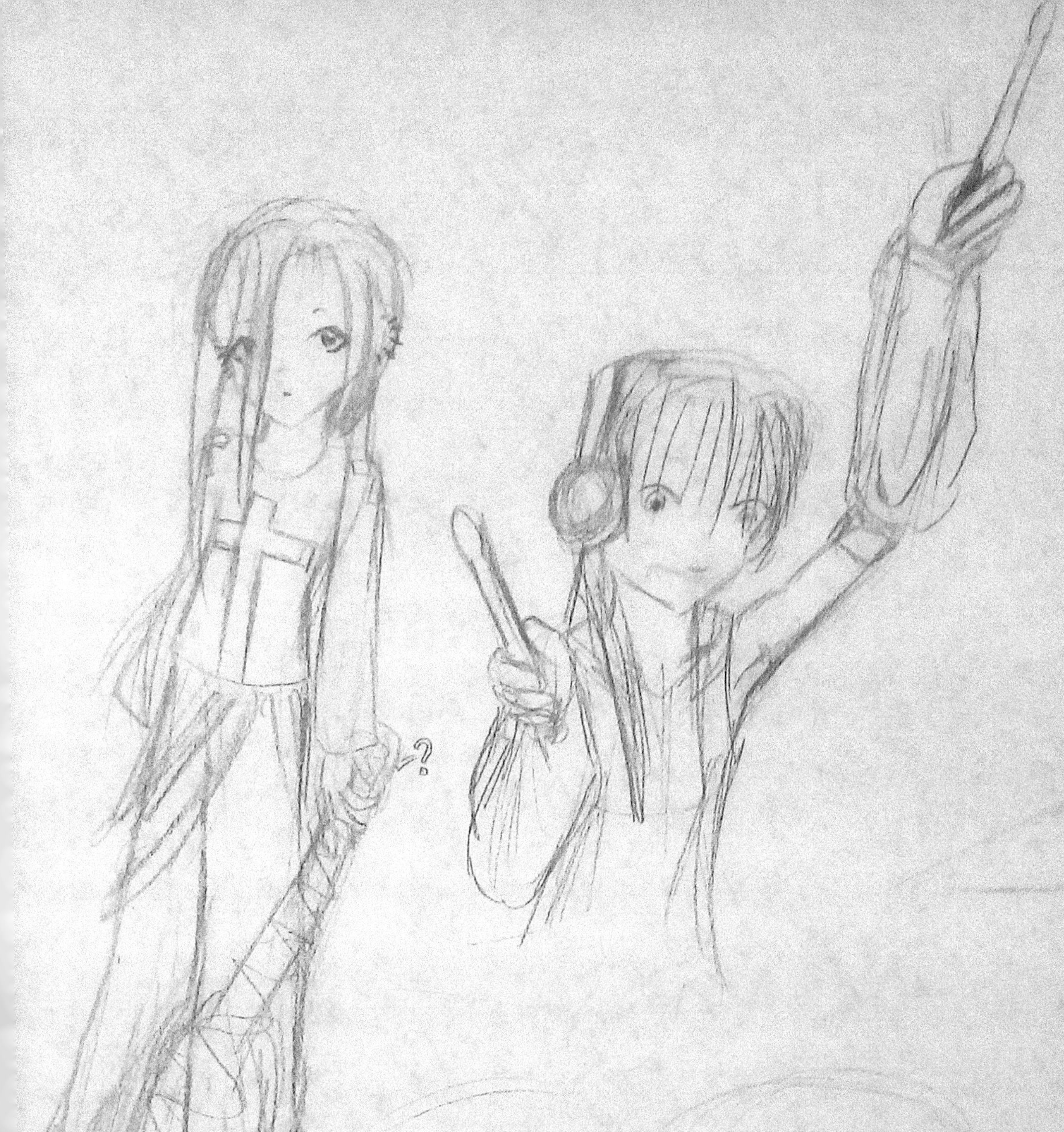

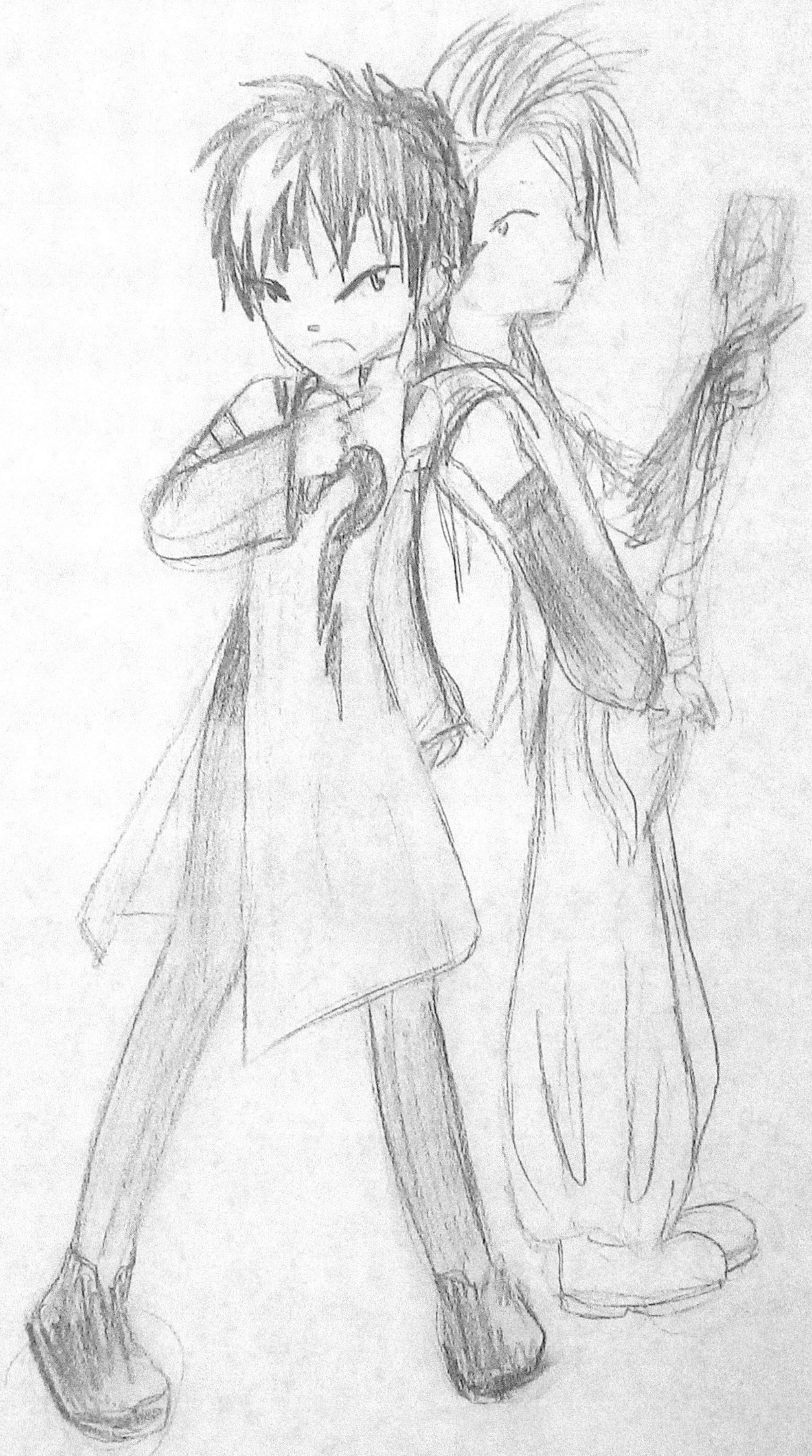

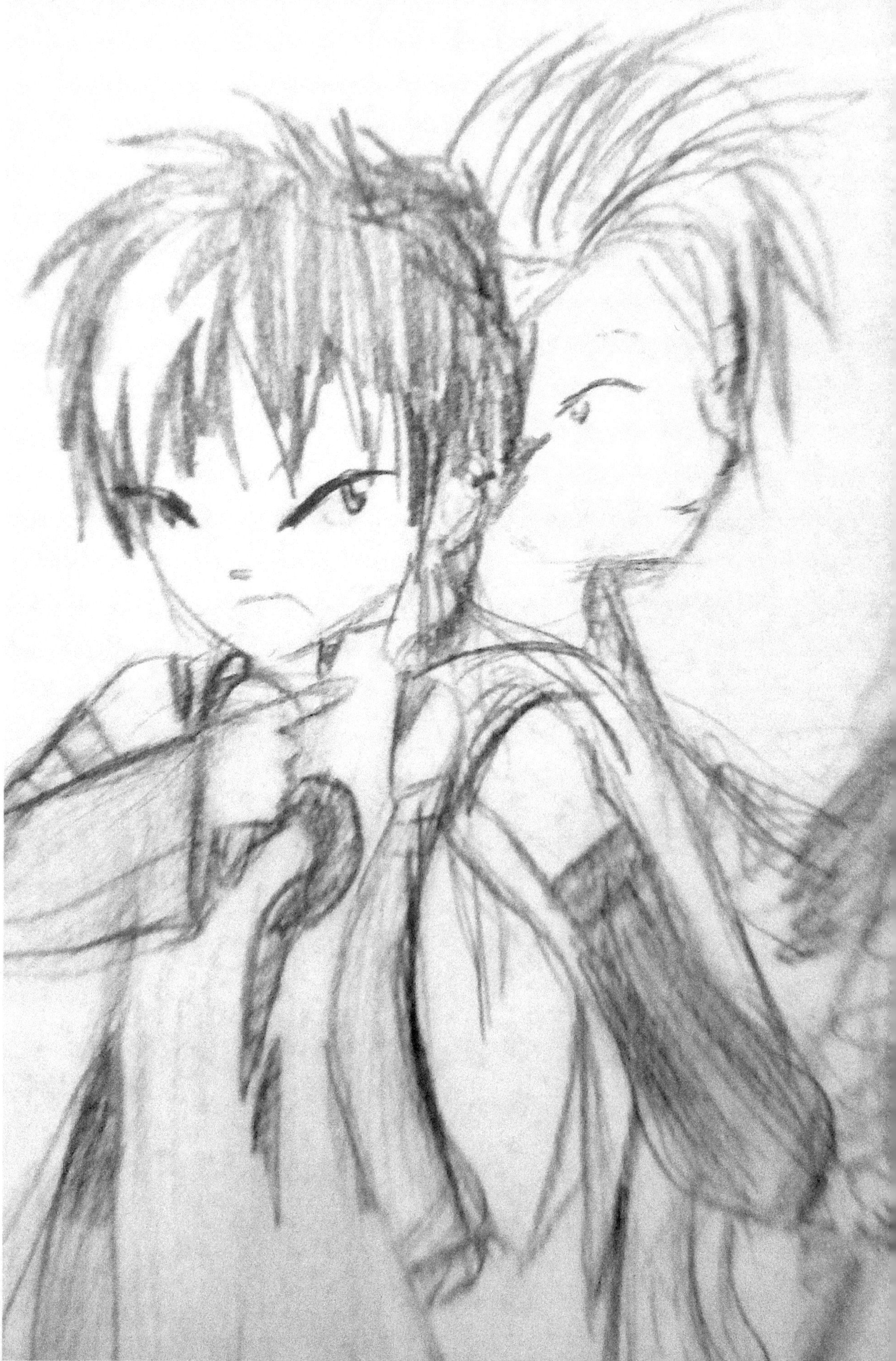

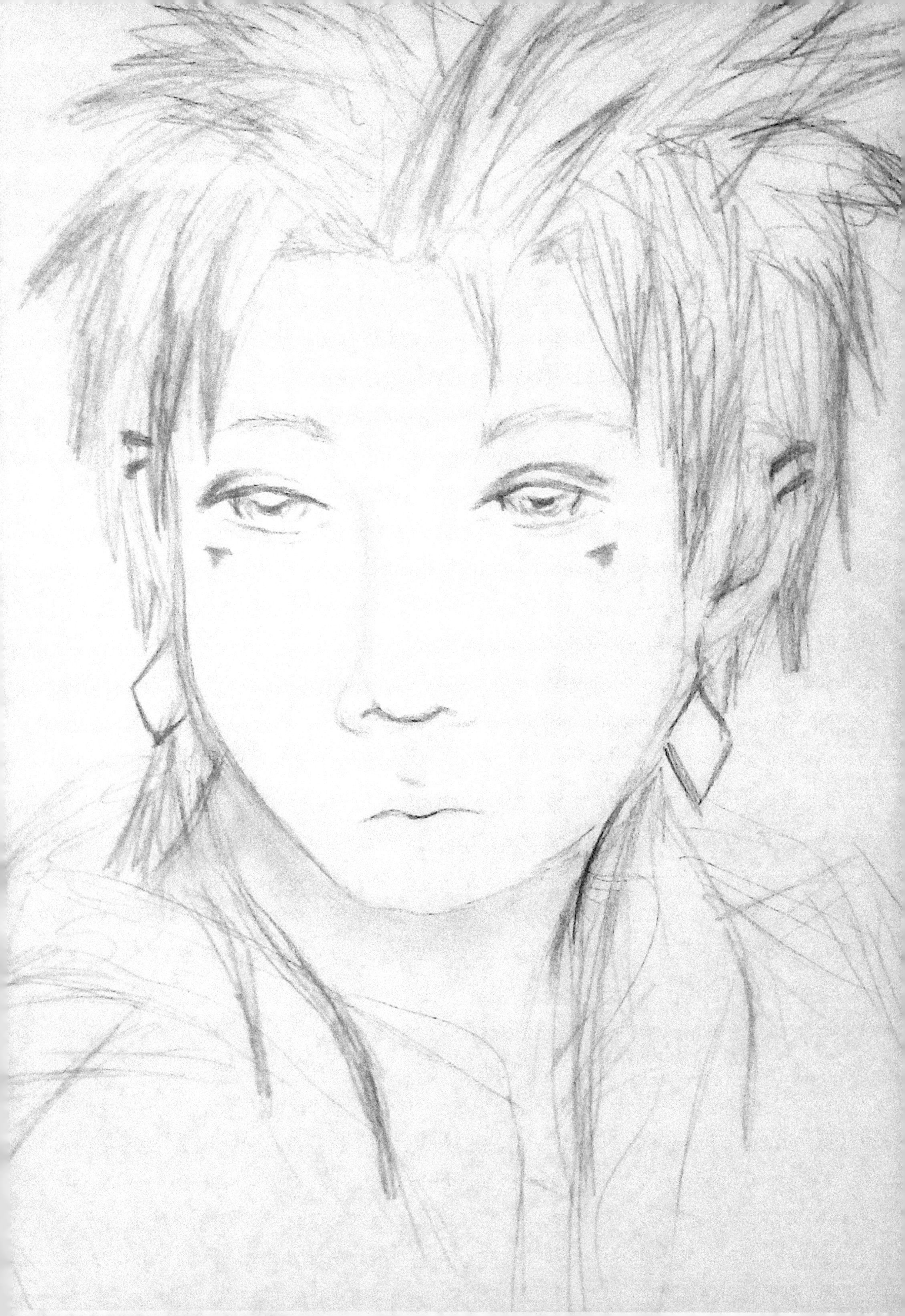

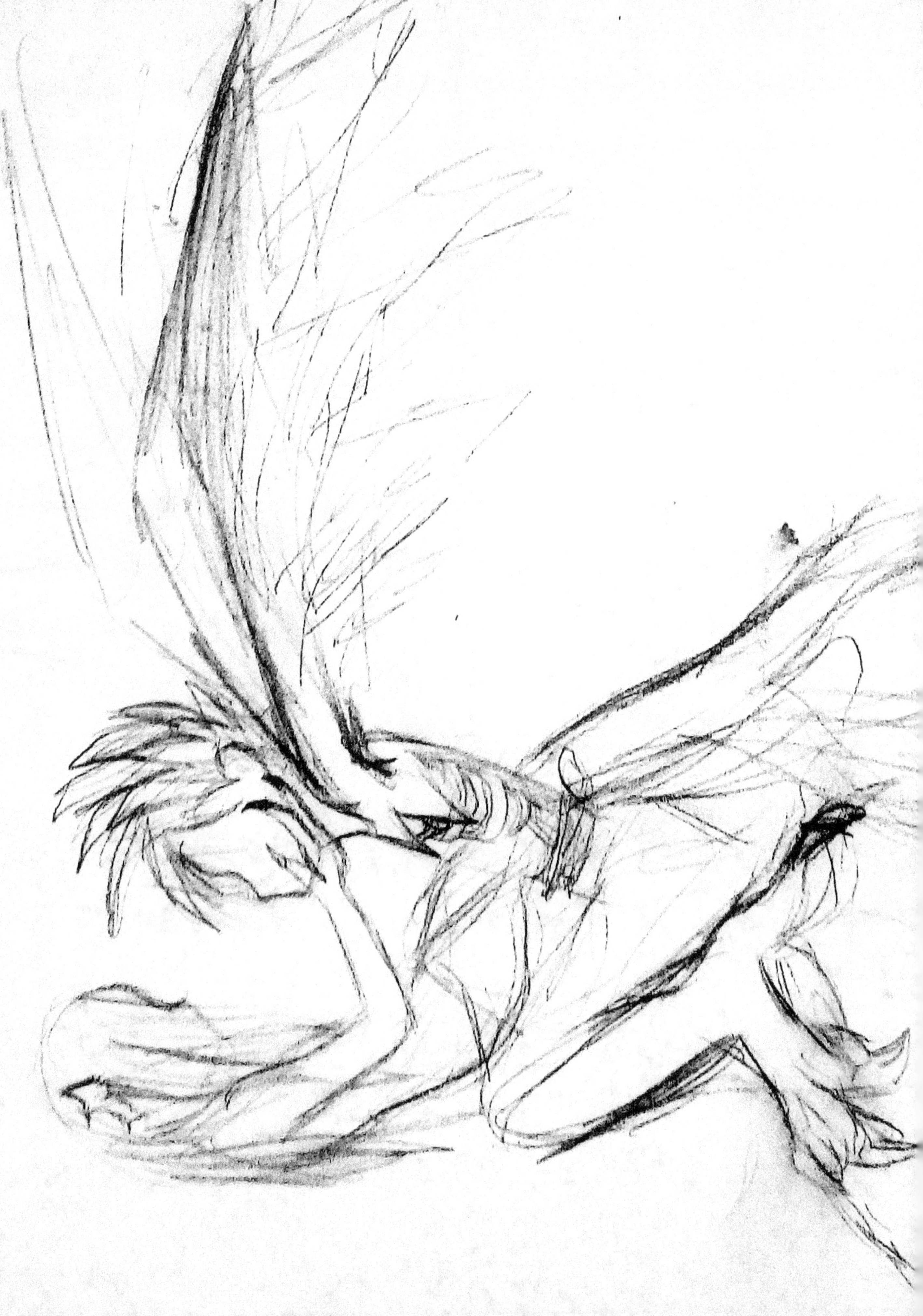

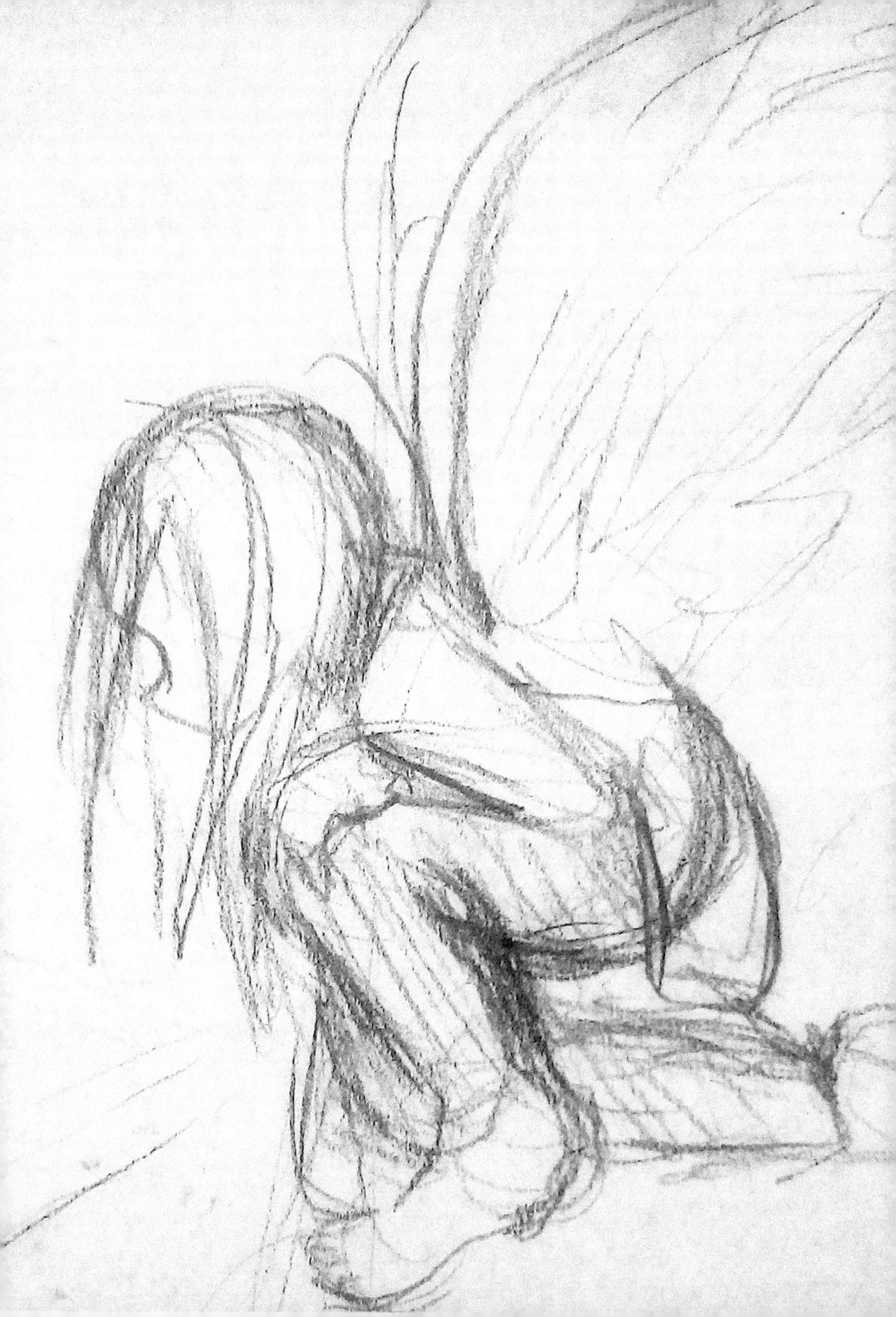

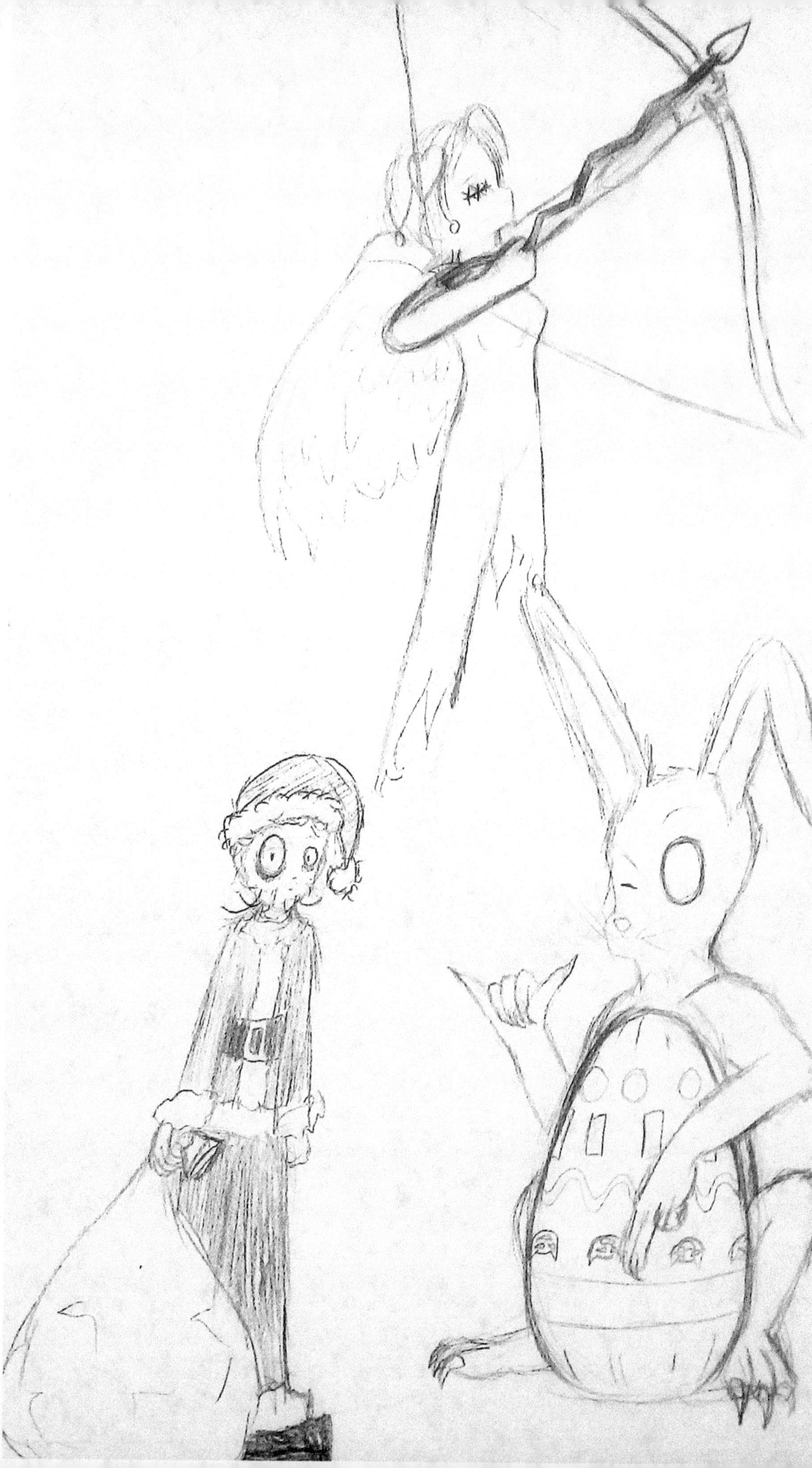

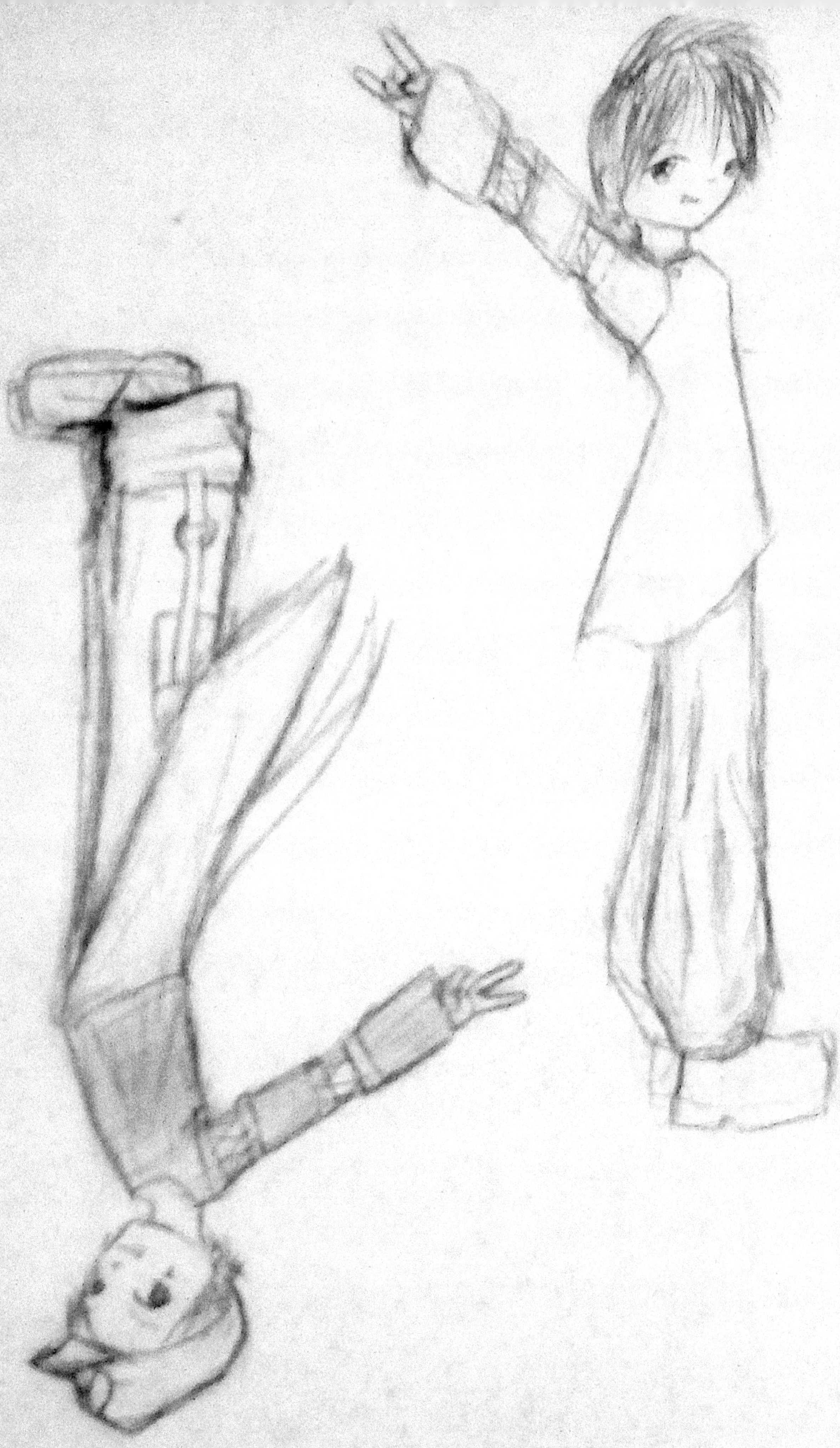

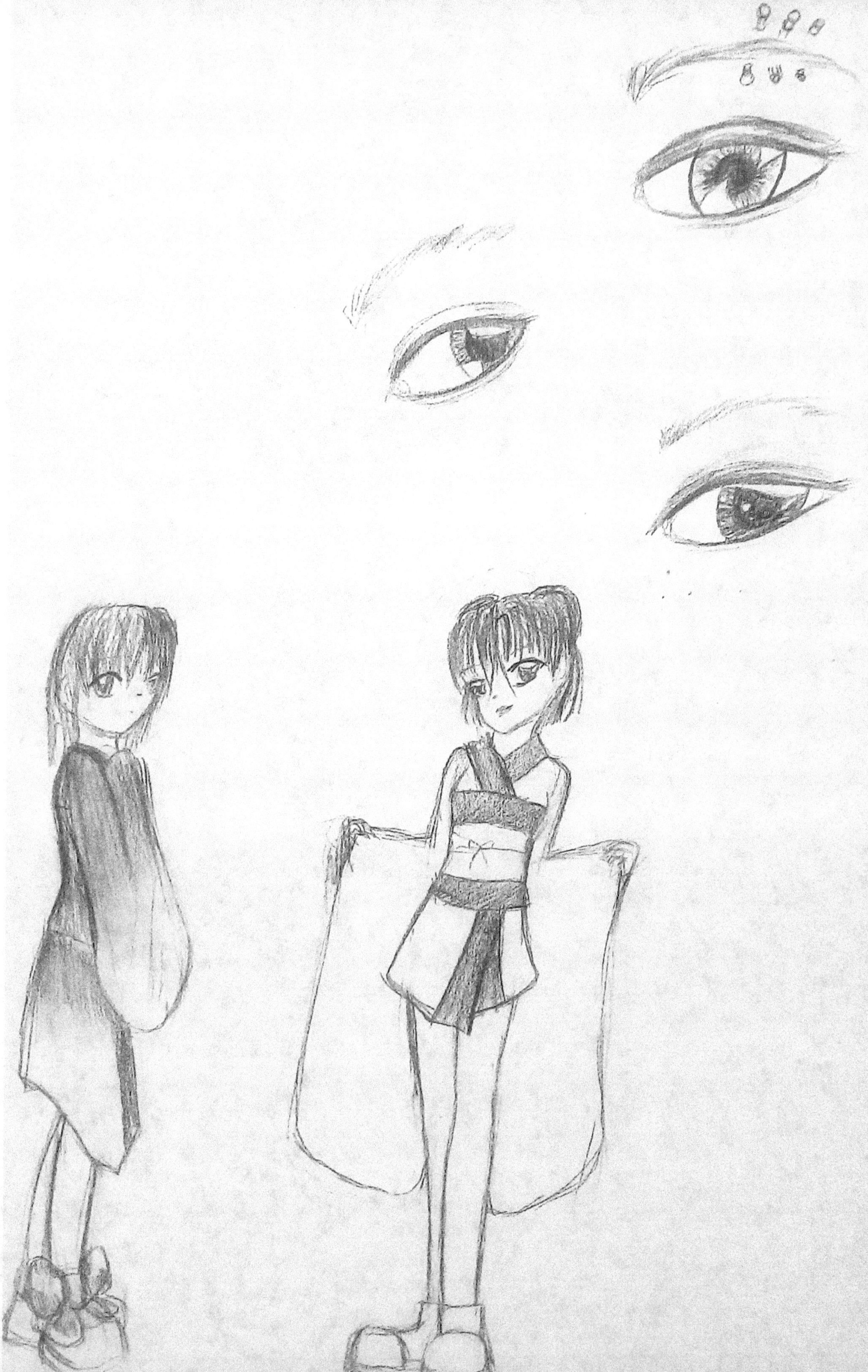

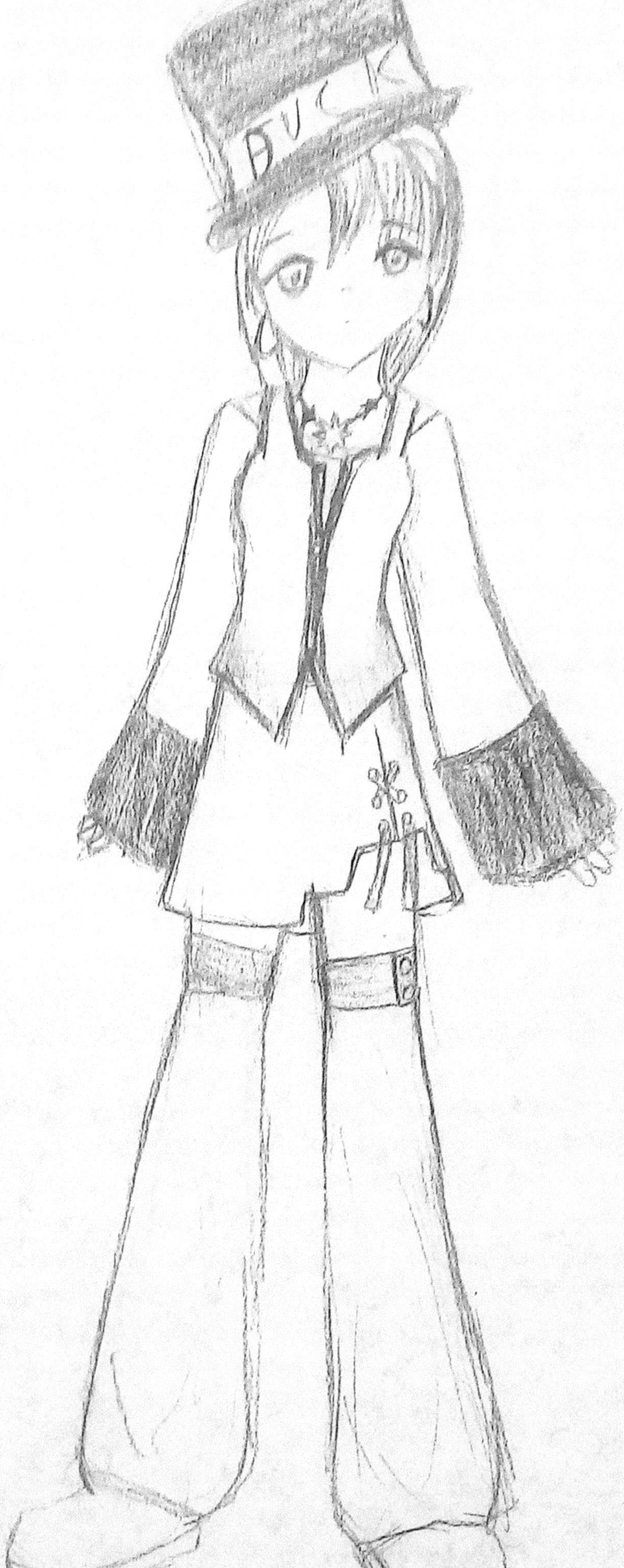
DUCK

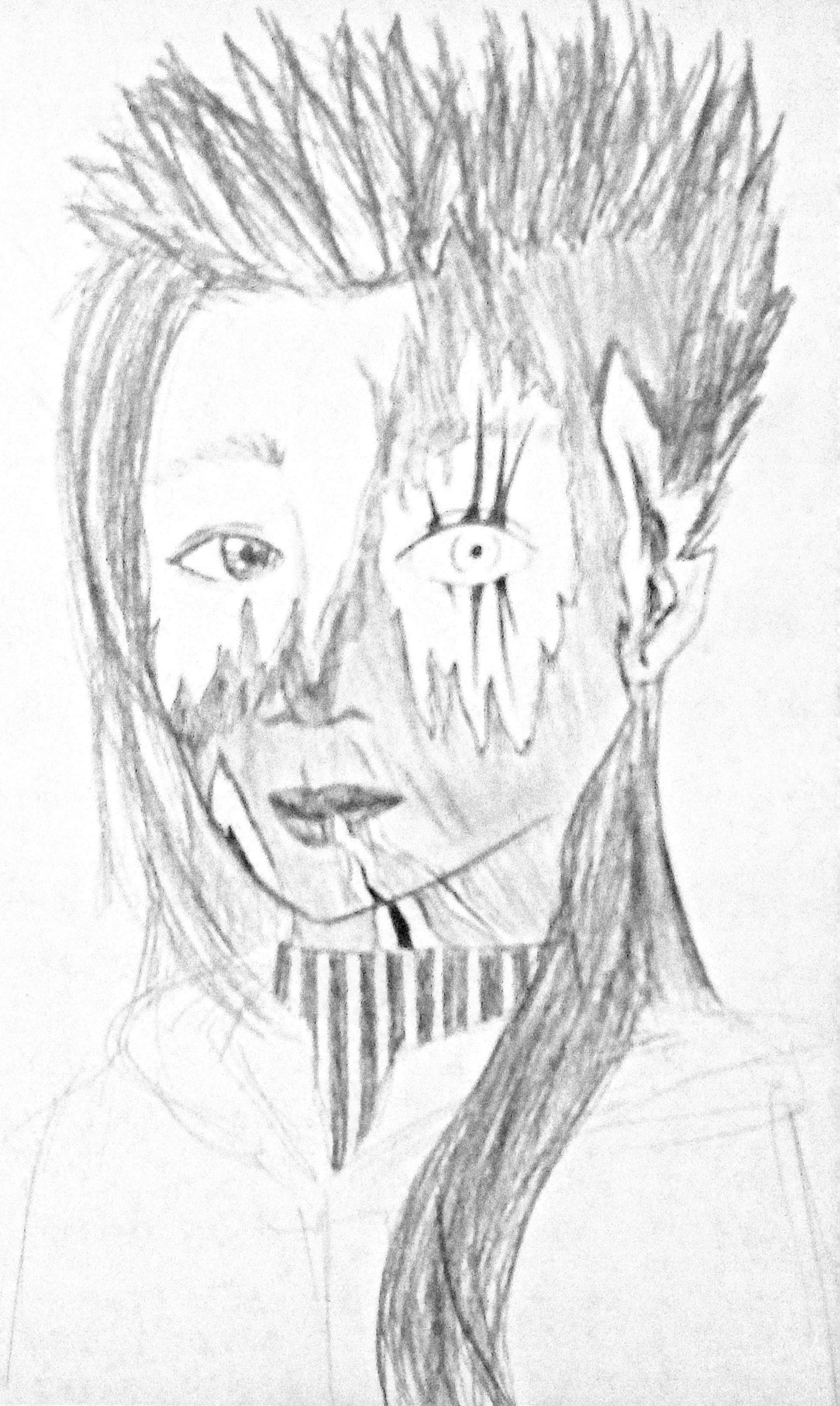

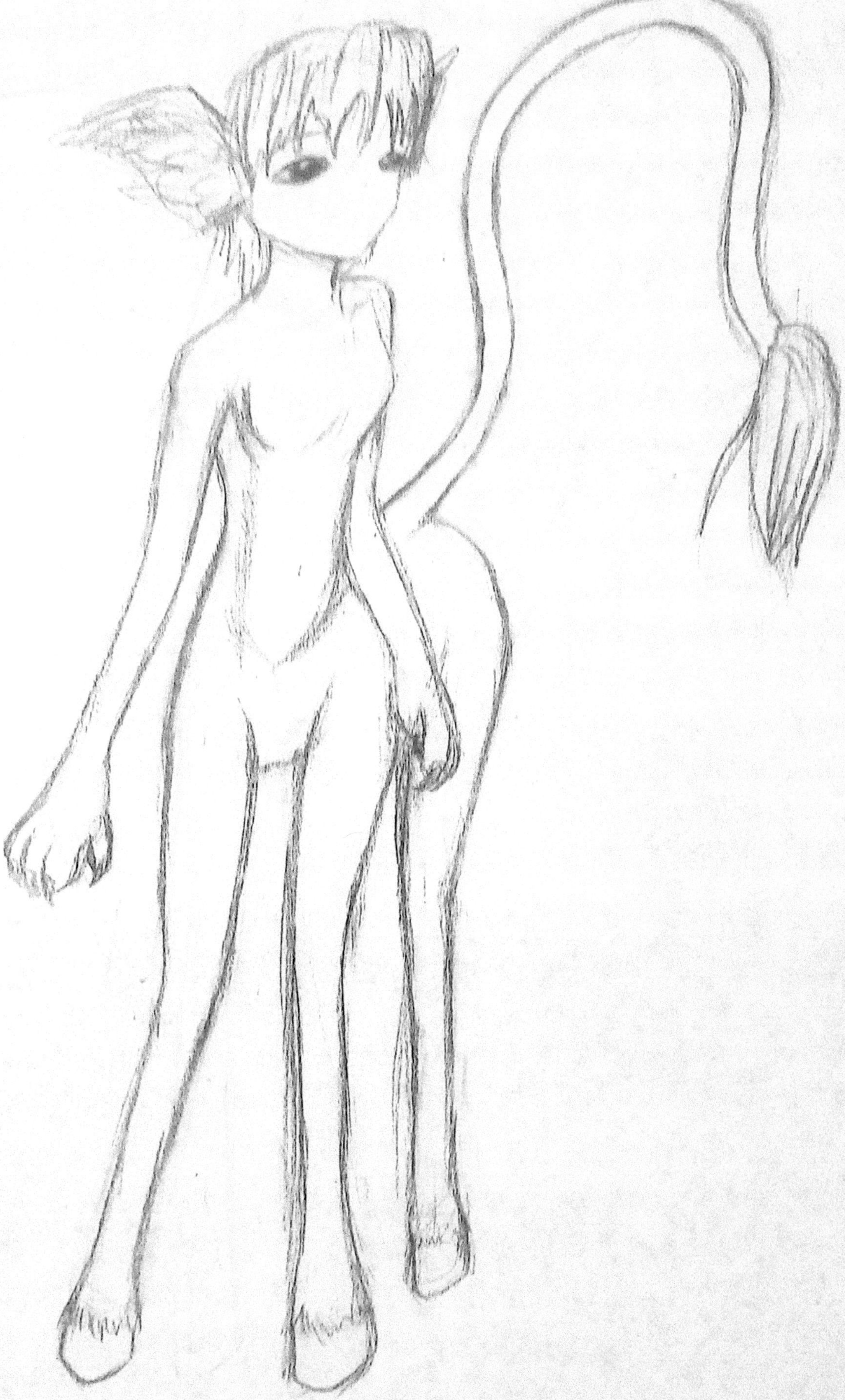

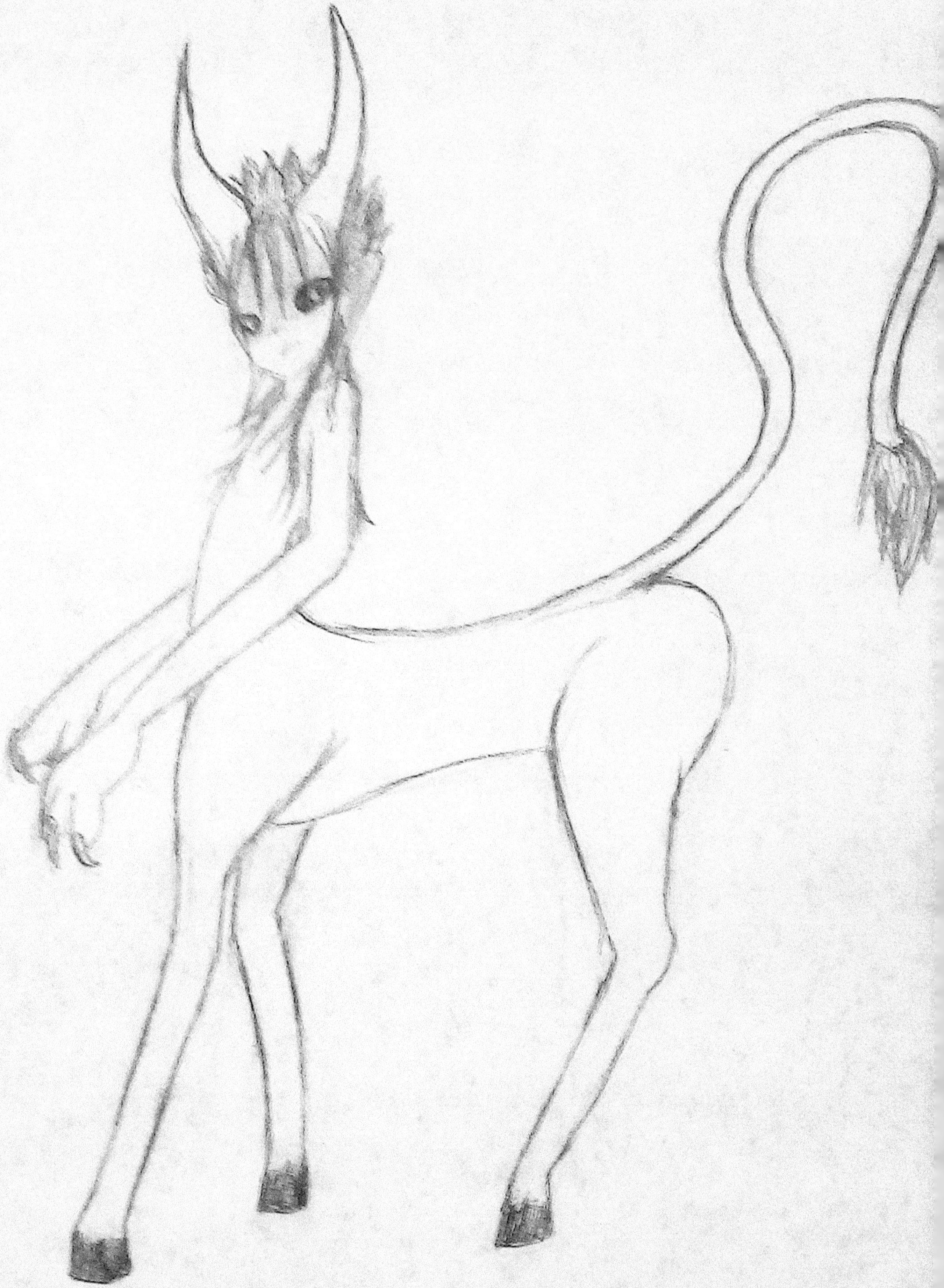

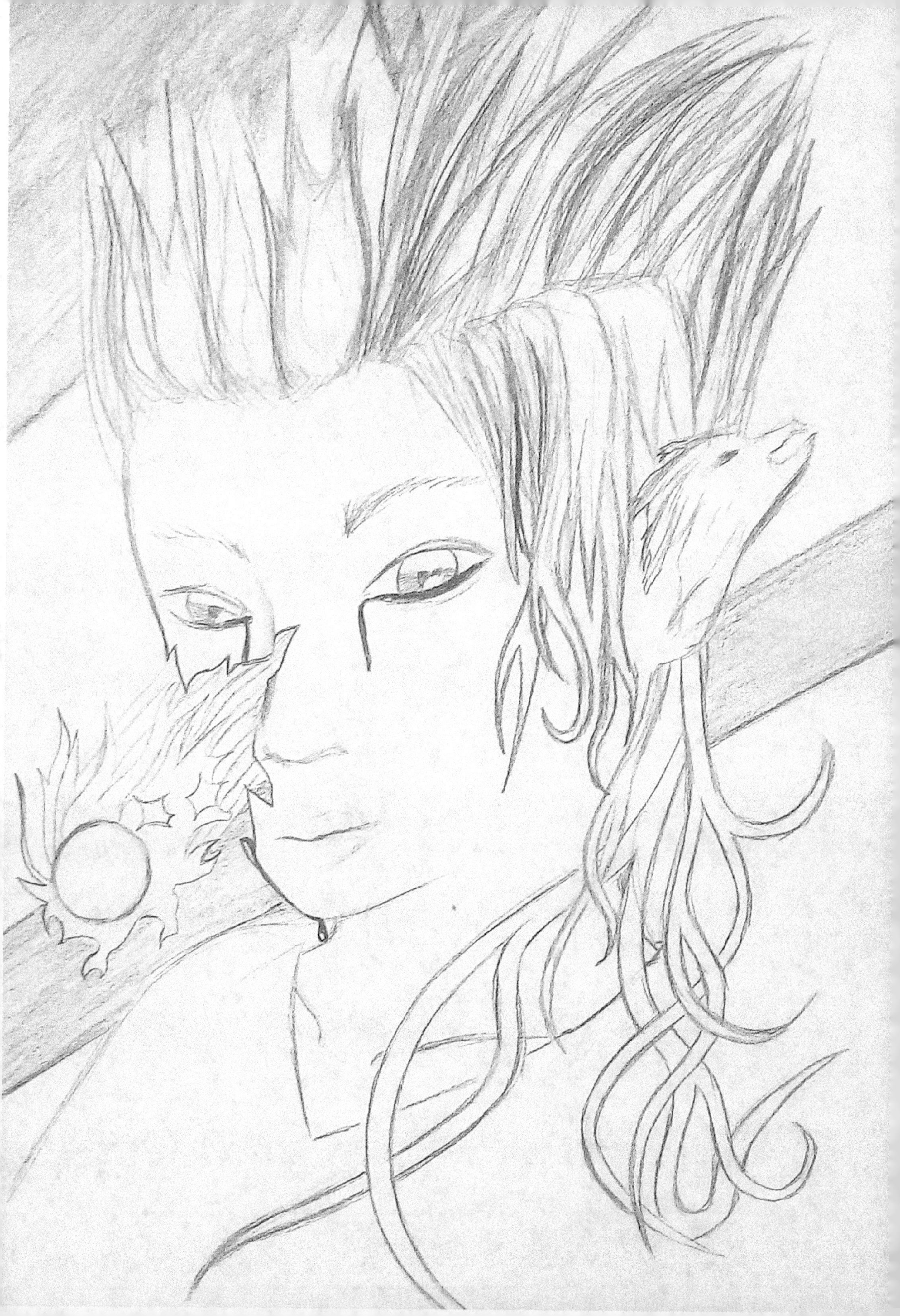

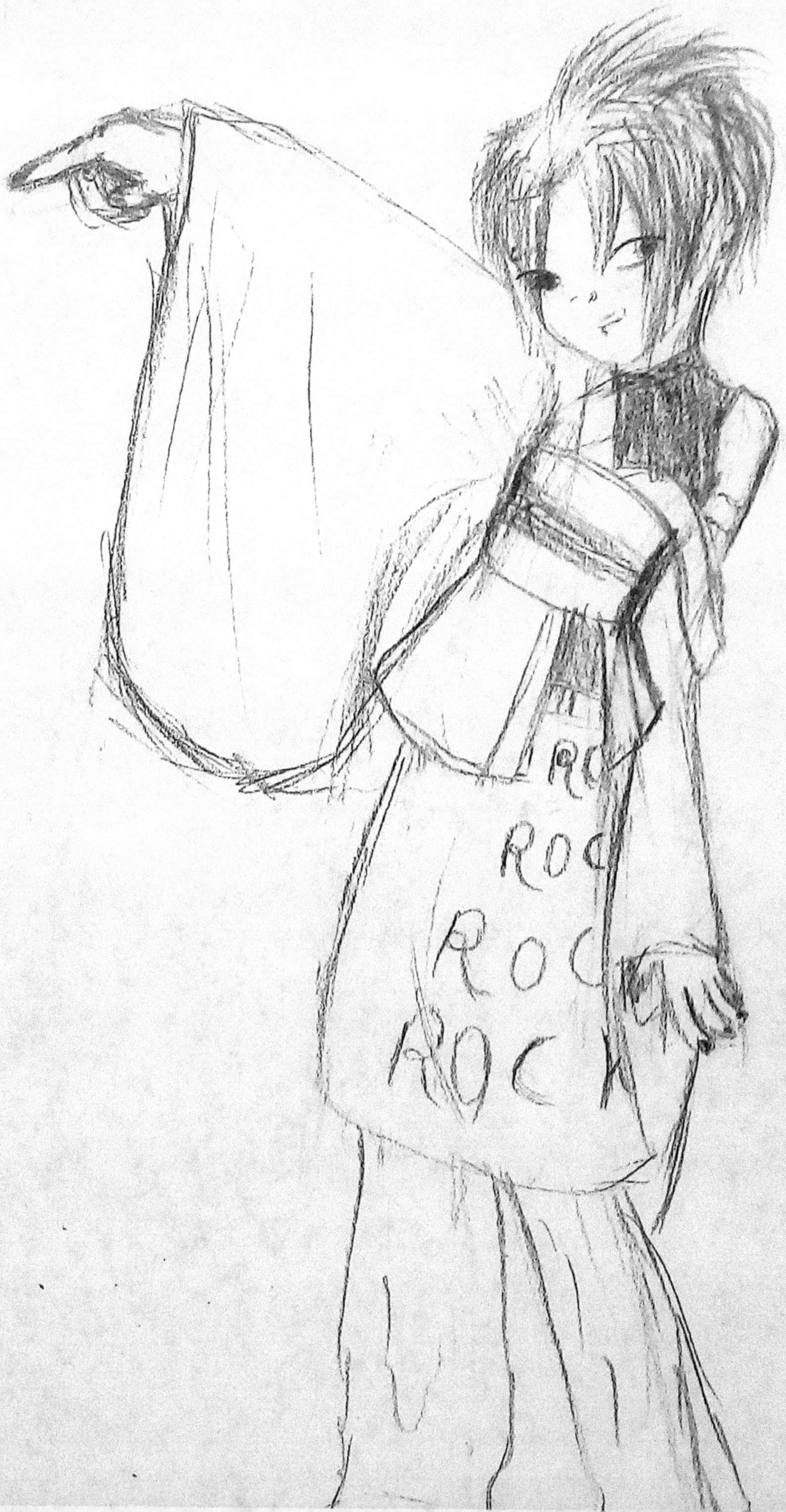
RO
ROC
ROC
ROCK

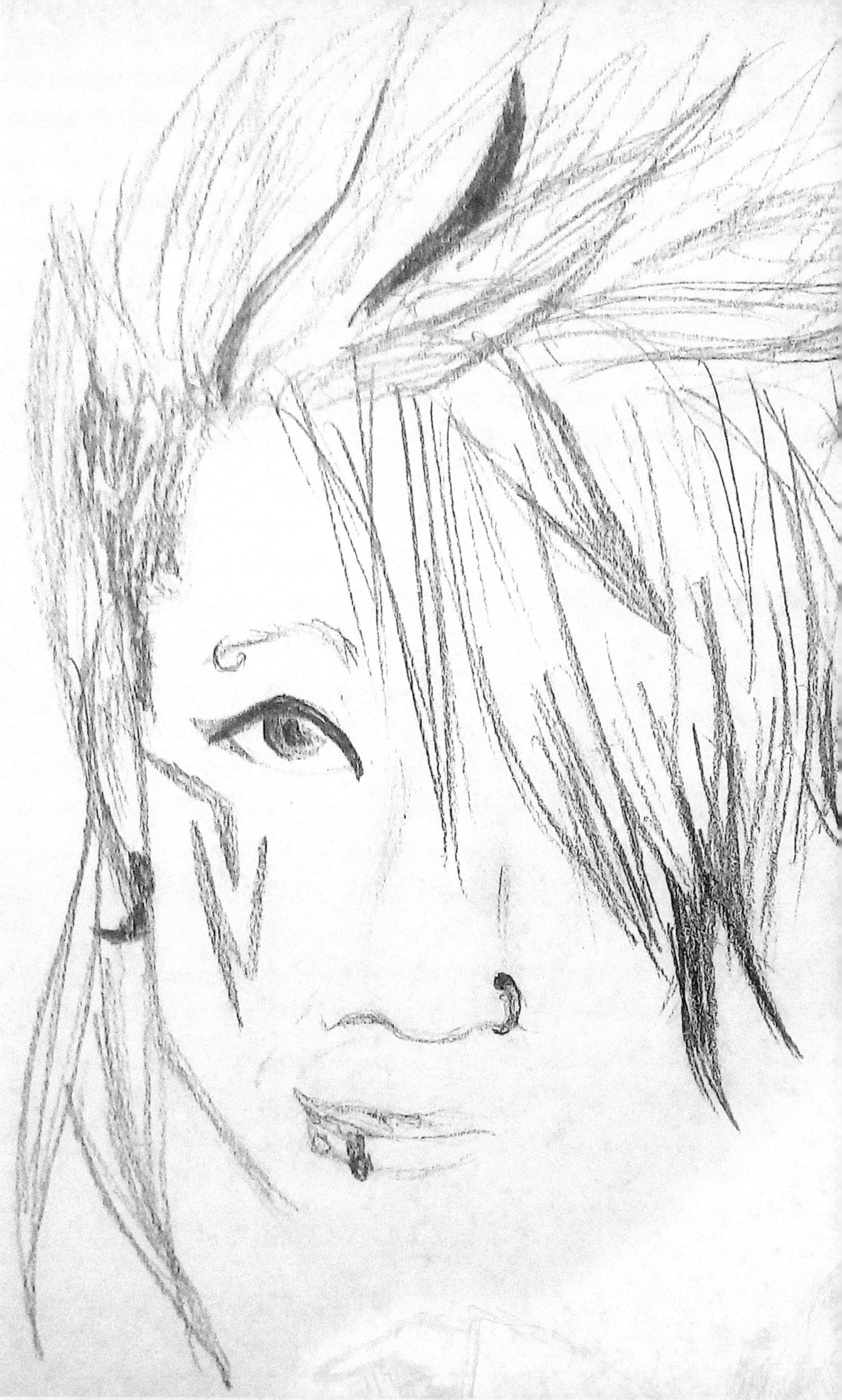

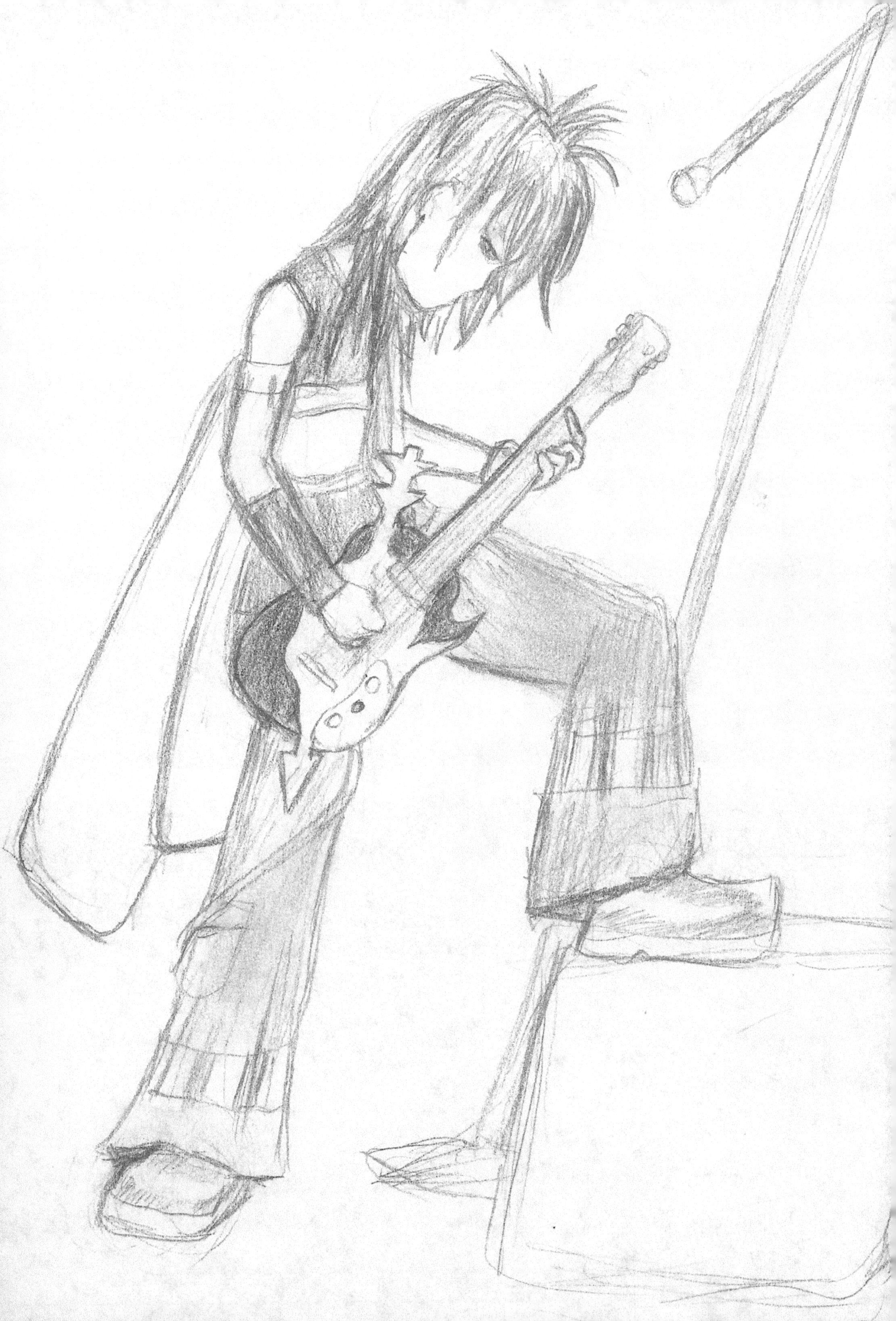

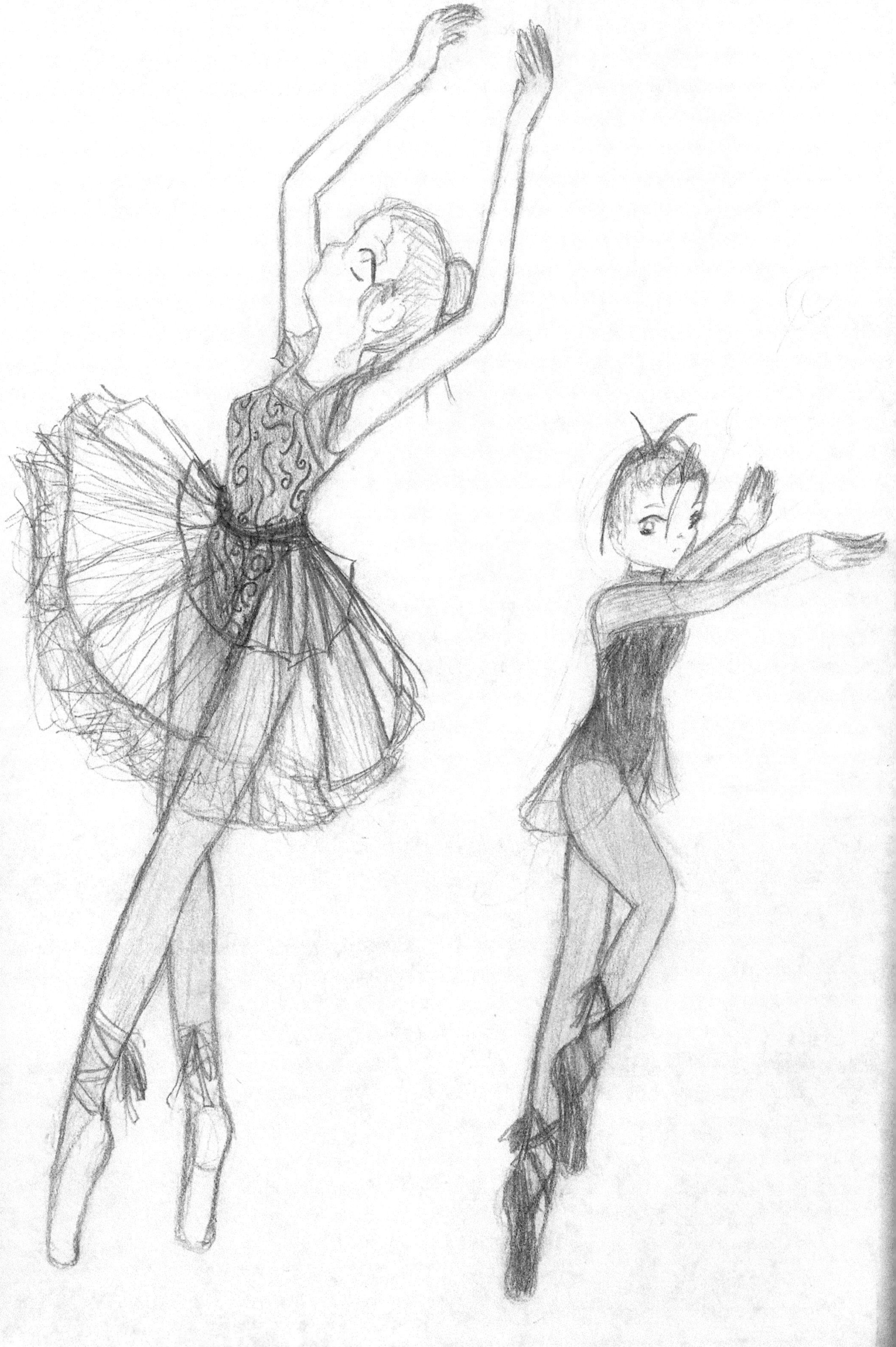

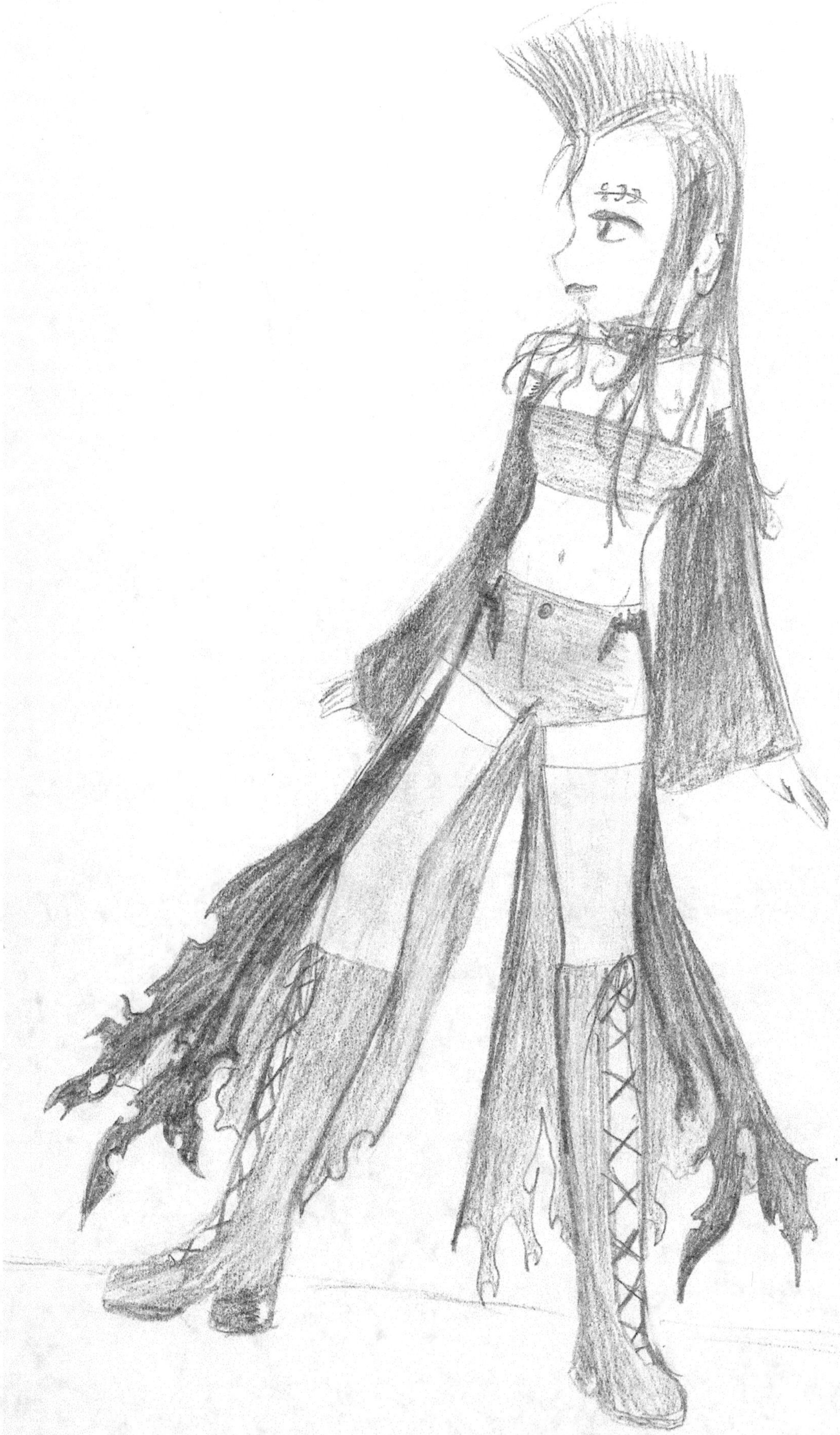

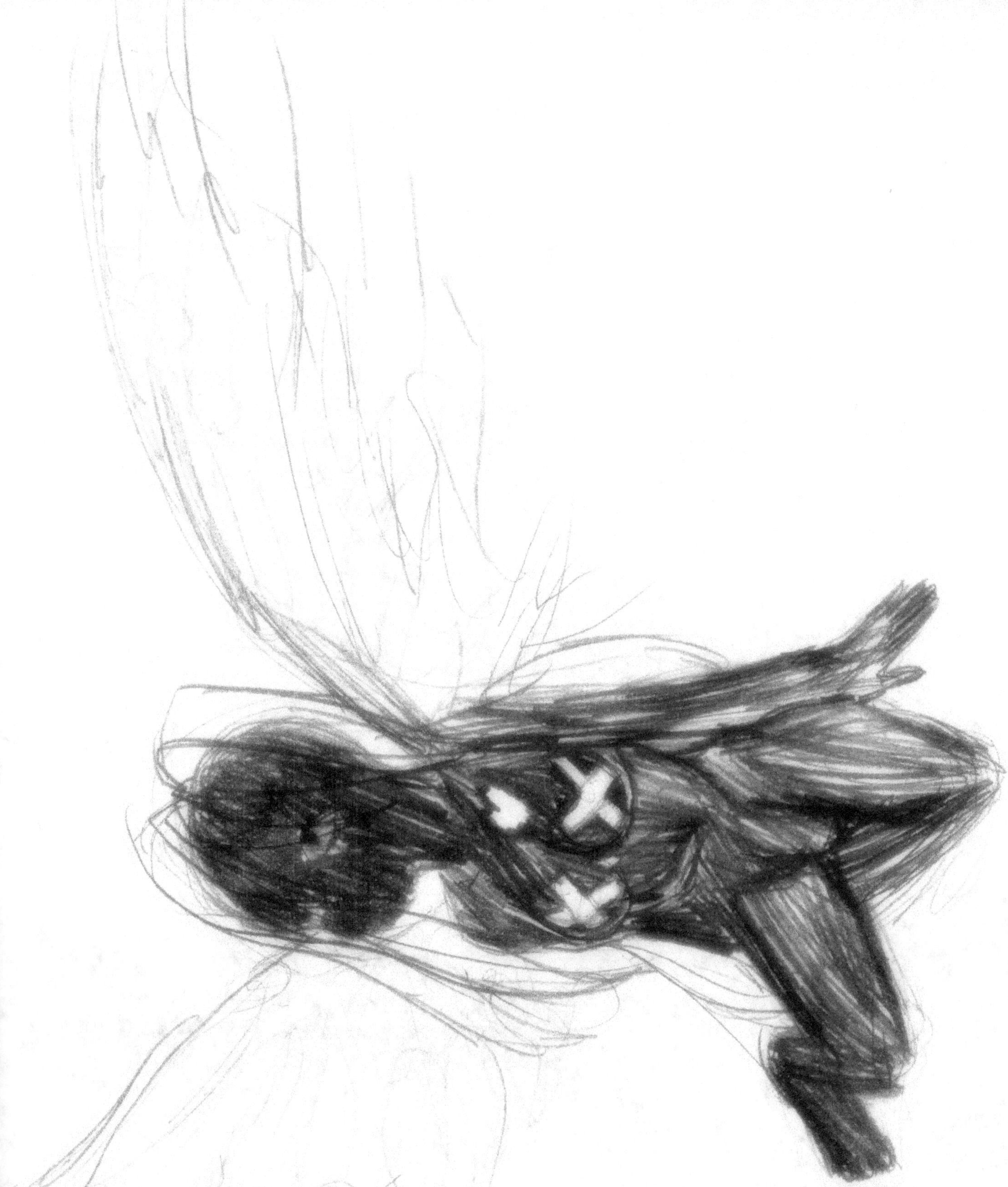

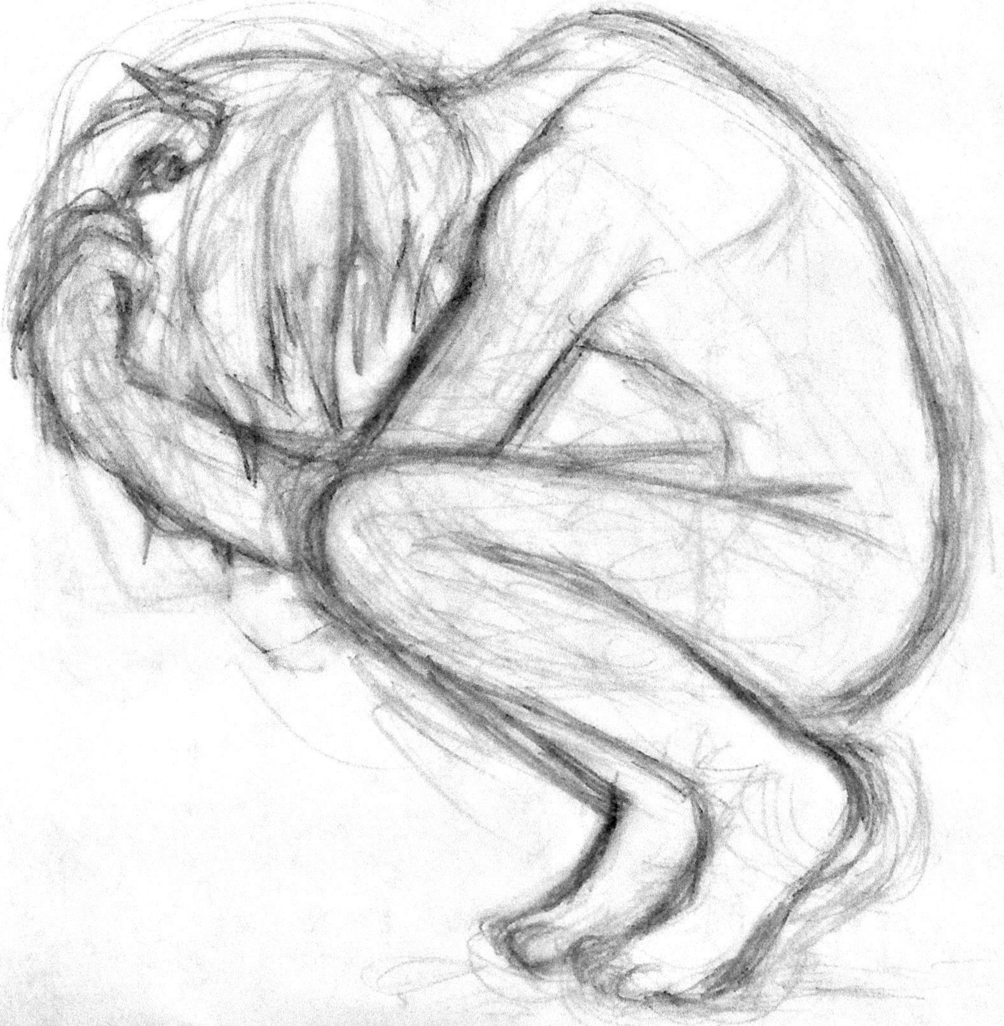

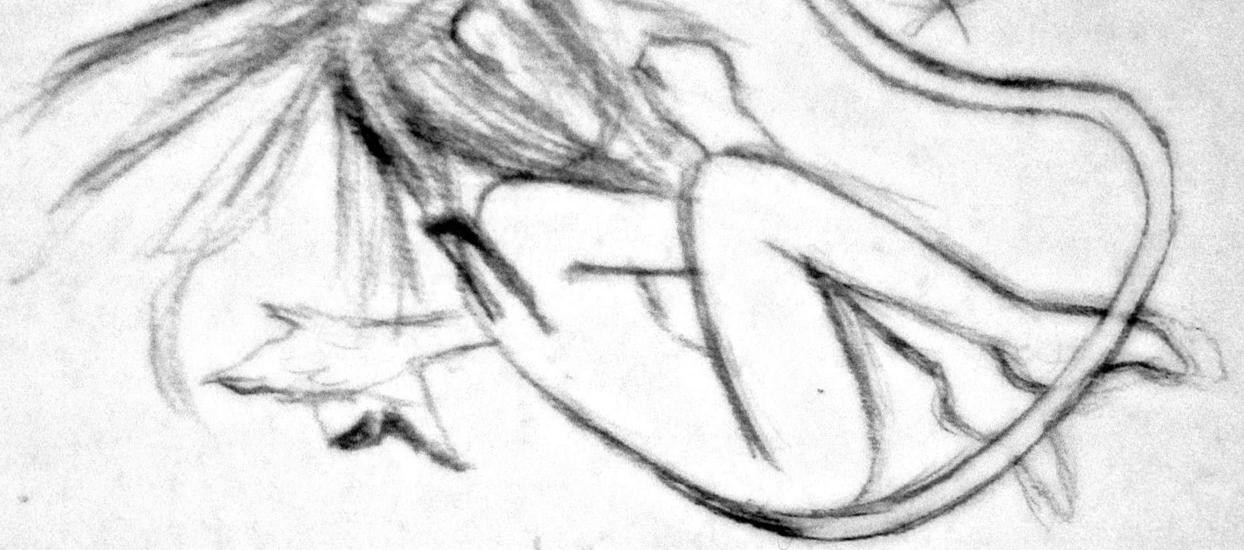

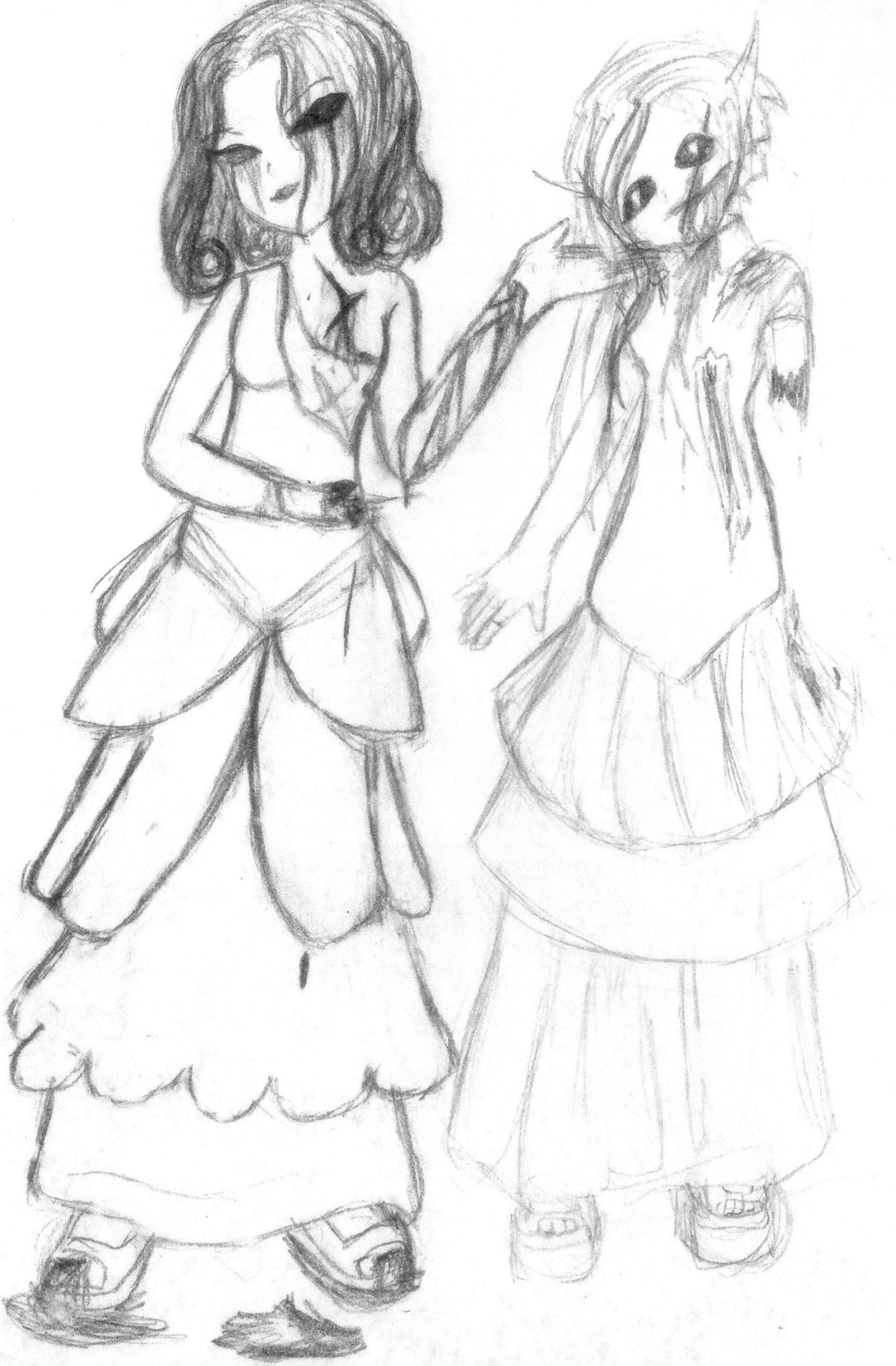

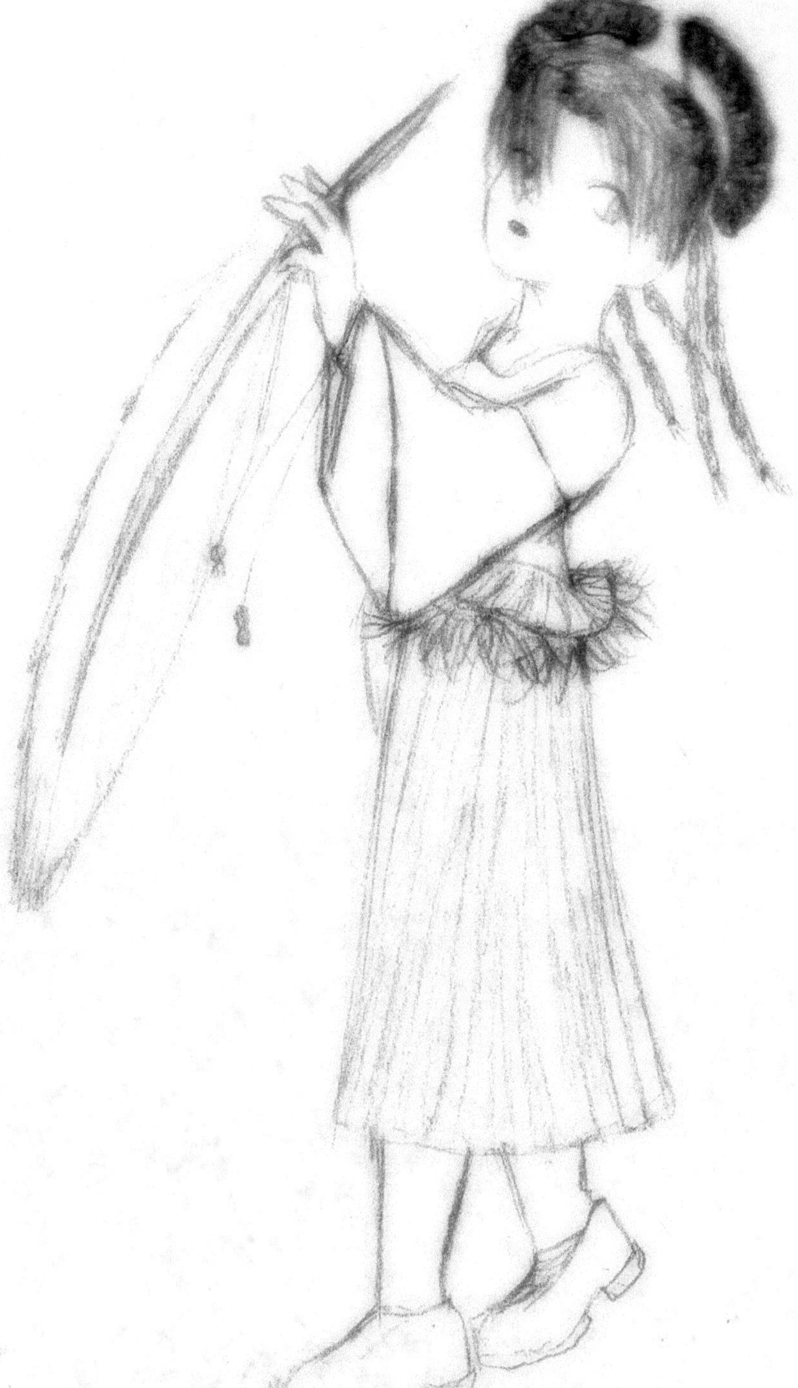

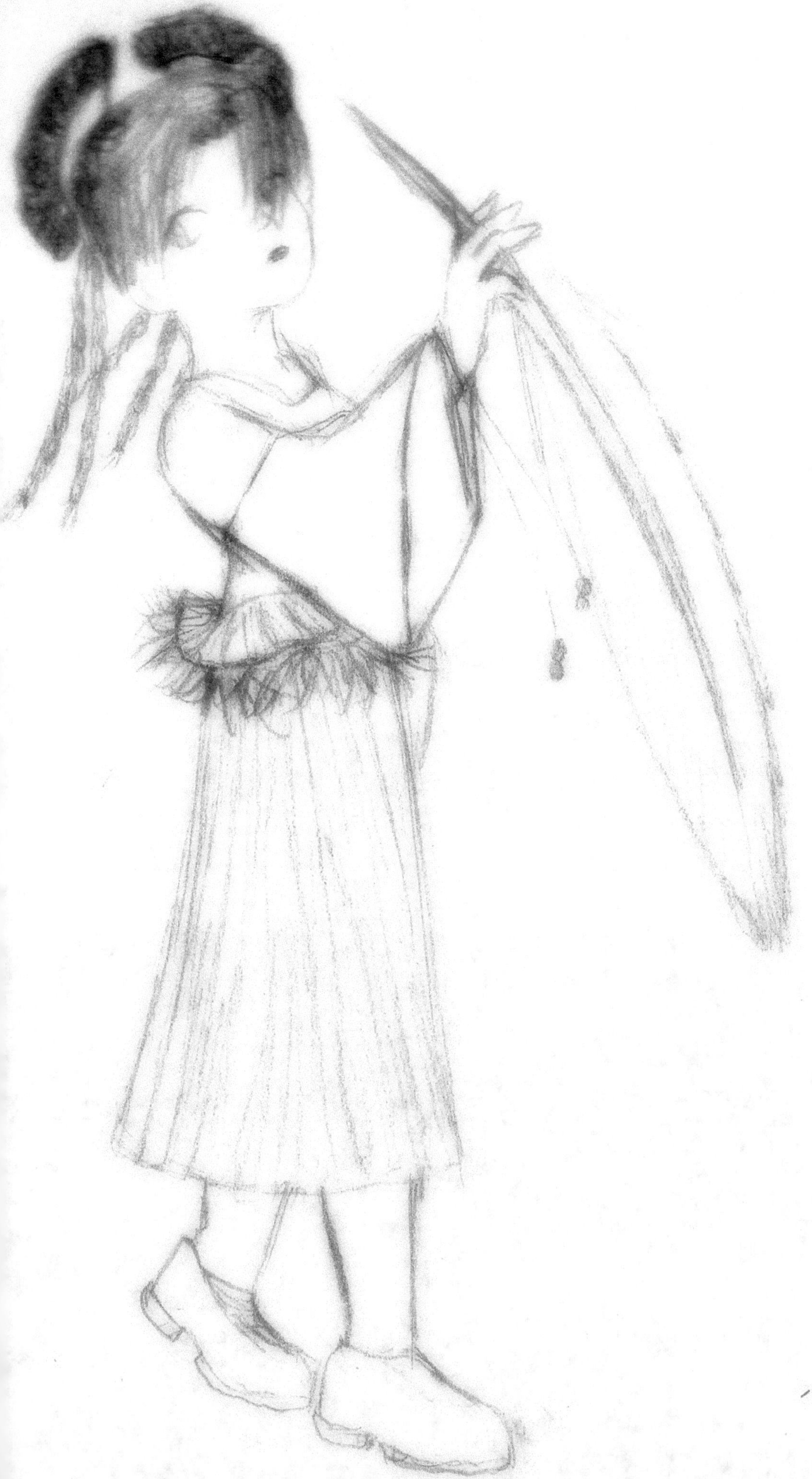

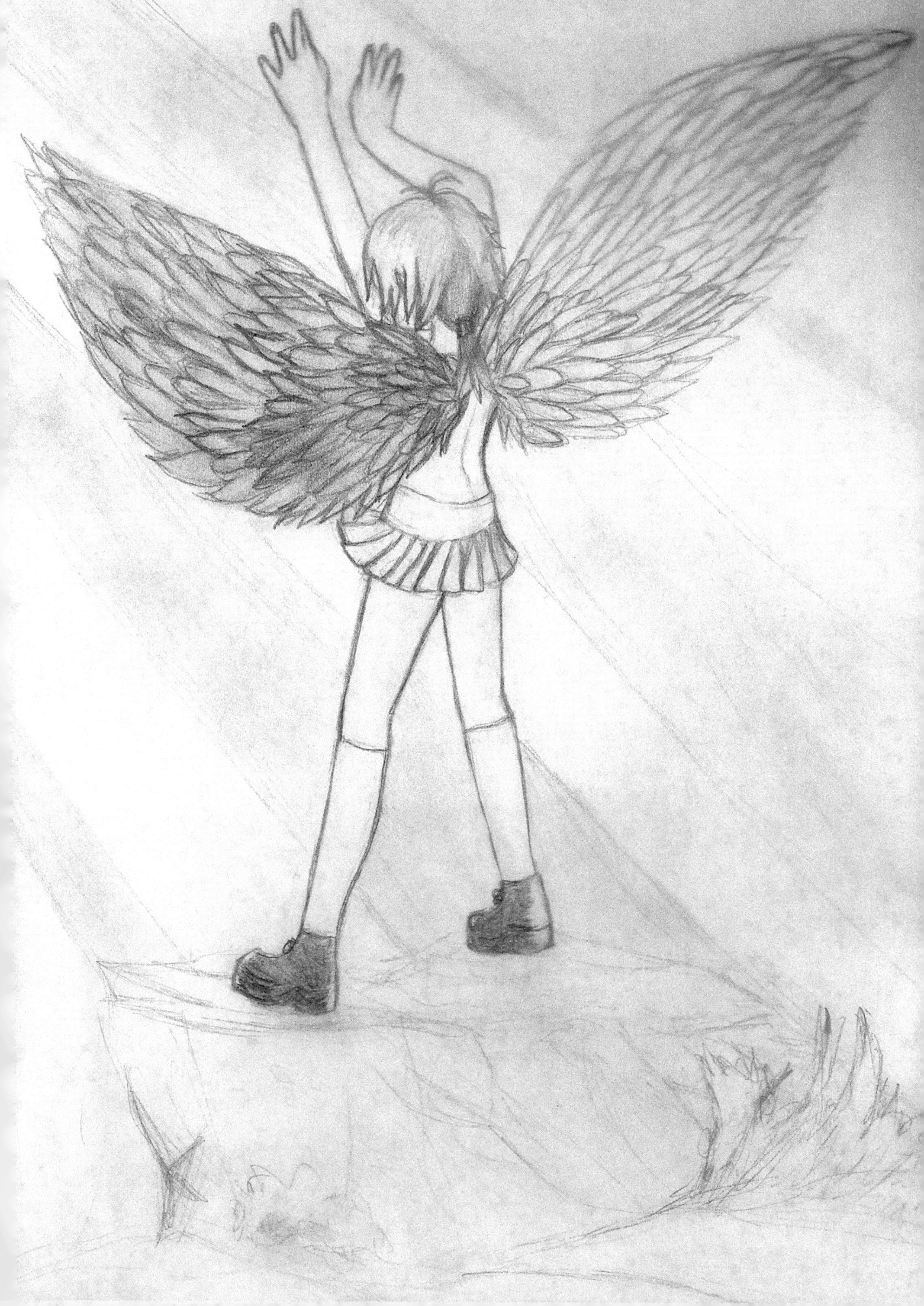

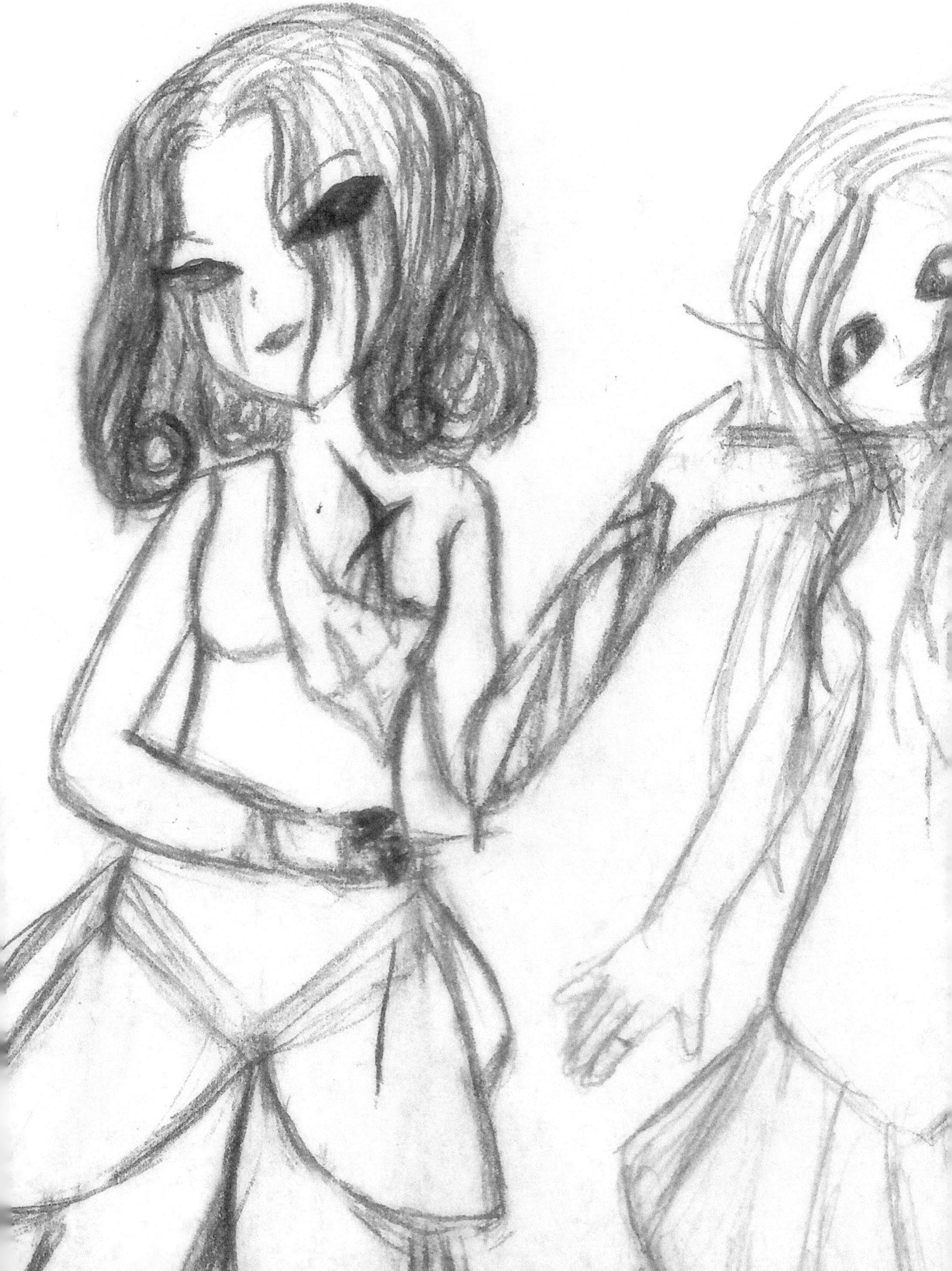

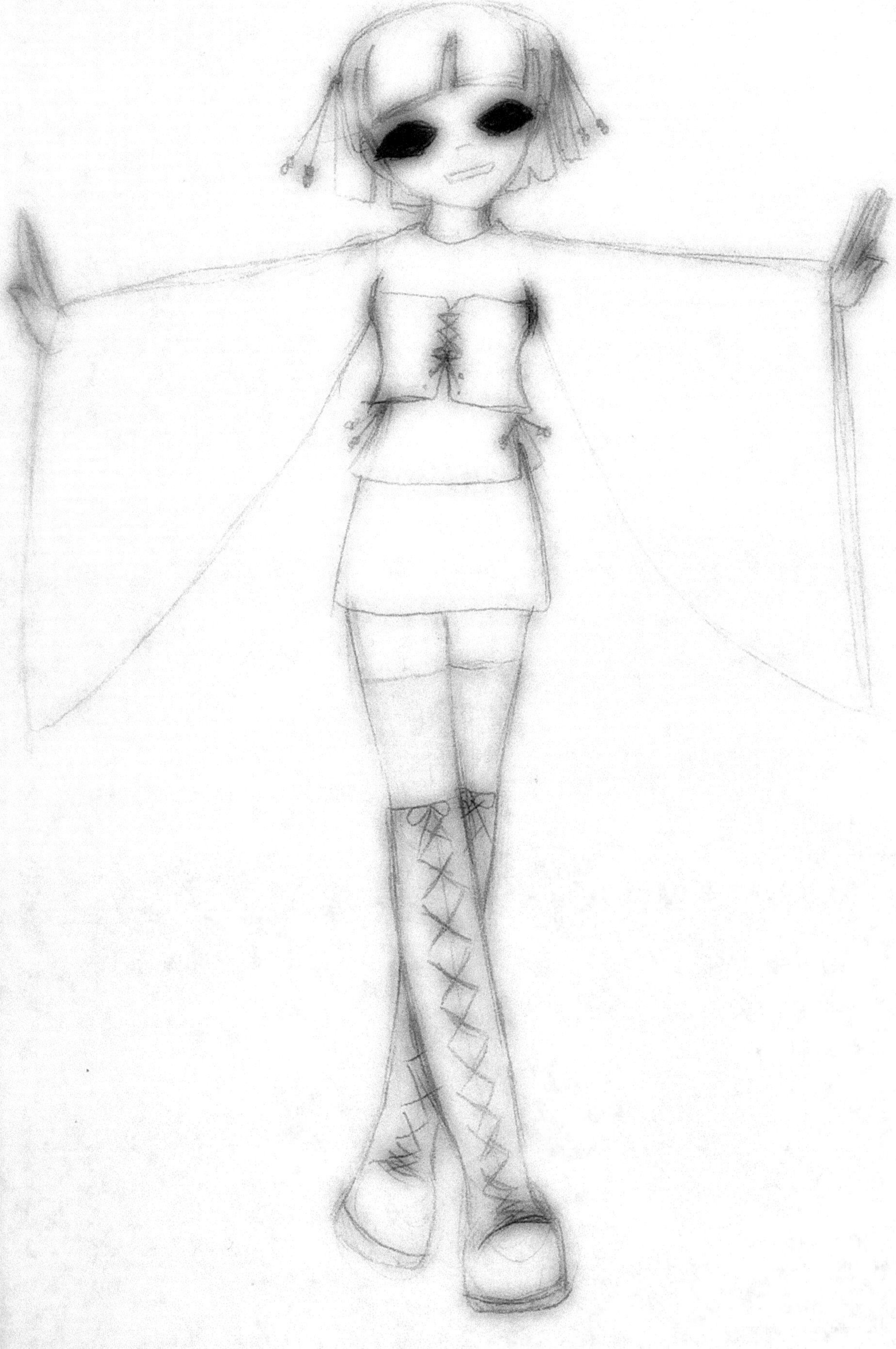

www.ingramcontent.com/pod-product-compliance
Lightning Source LLC
Chambersburg PA
CBHW081203180526
45170CB00006B/2198
* 9 7 8 0 3 5 9 2 4 4 0 5 8 *